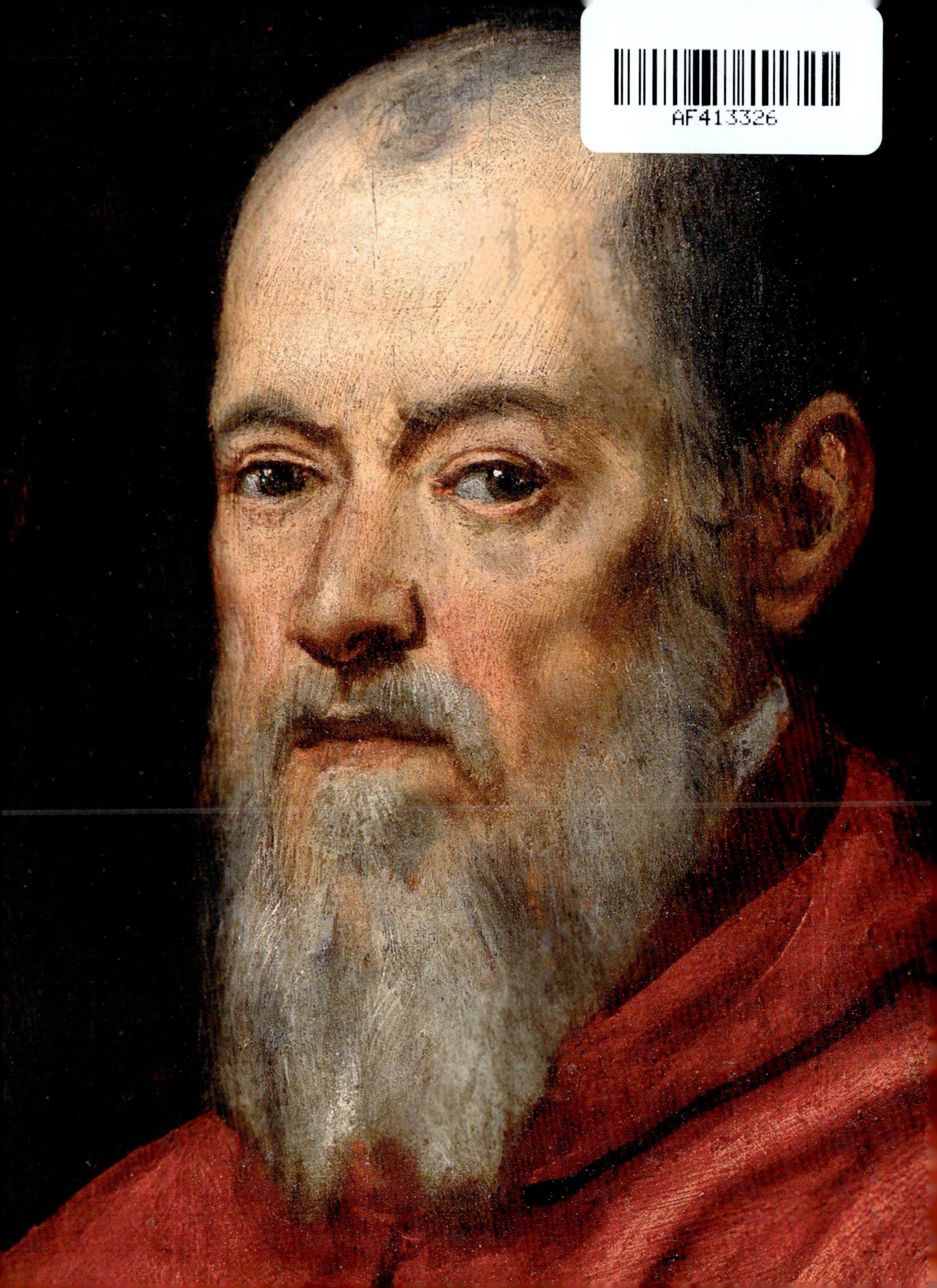
AF413326

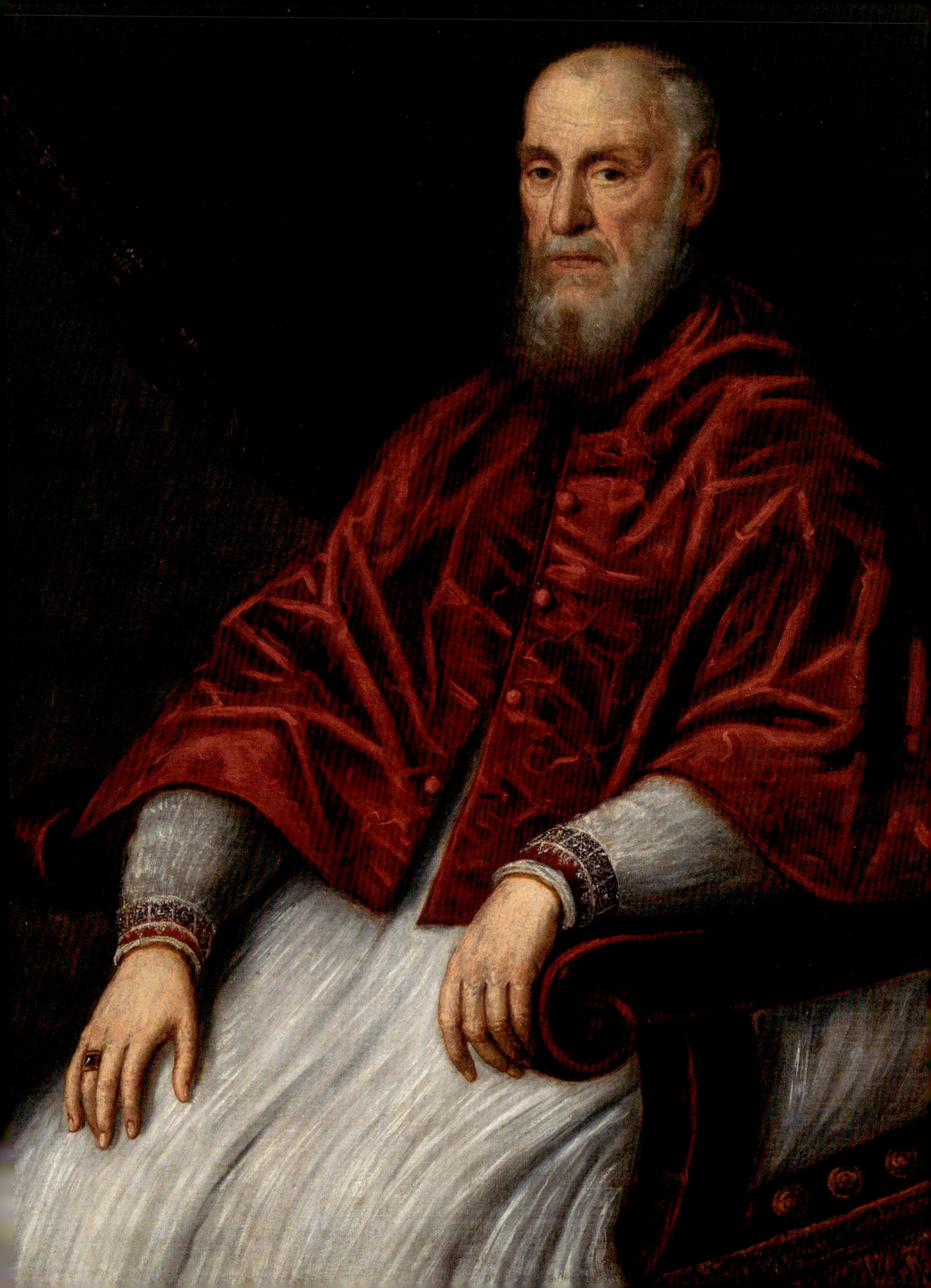

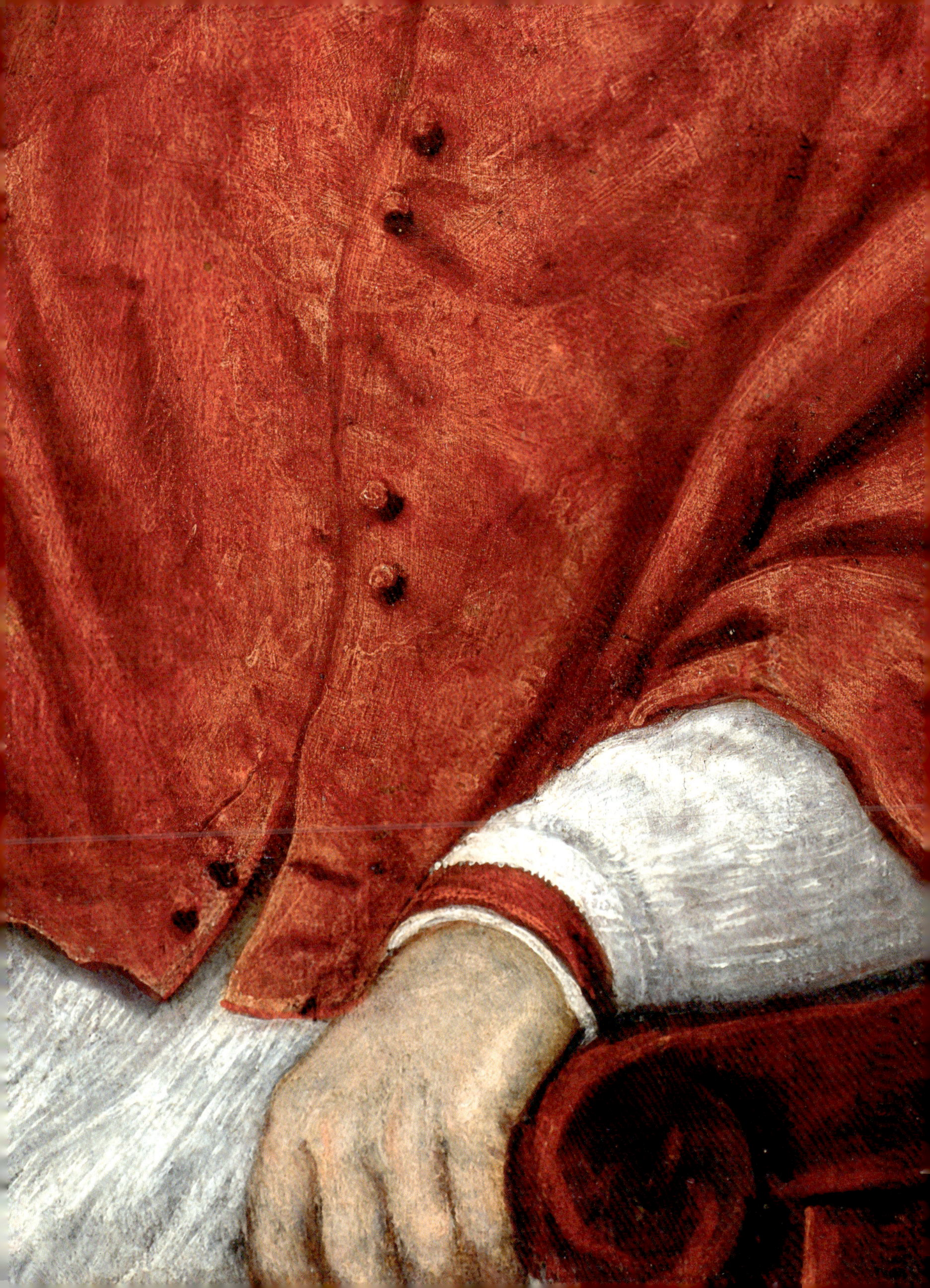

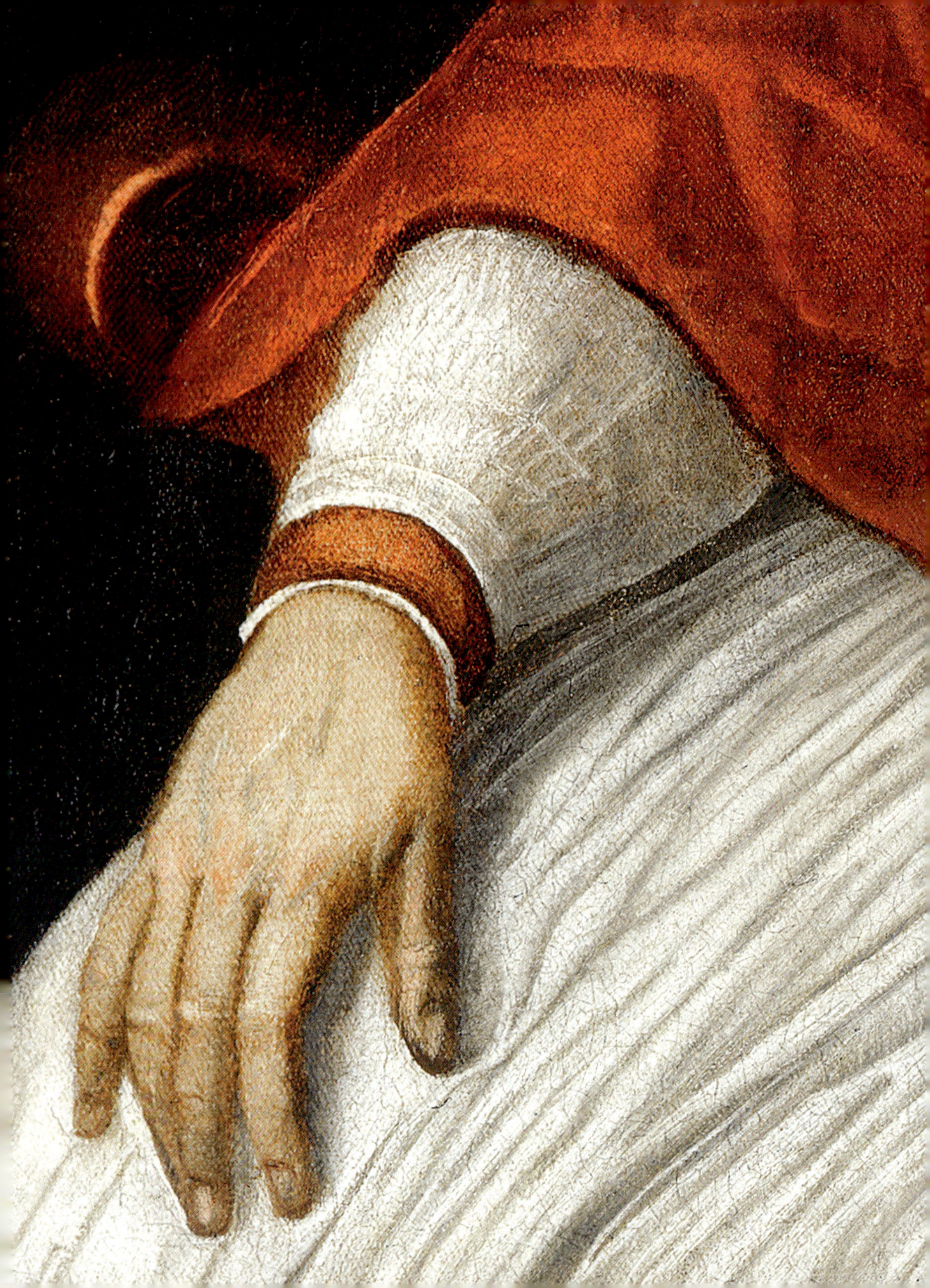

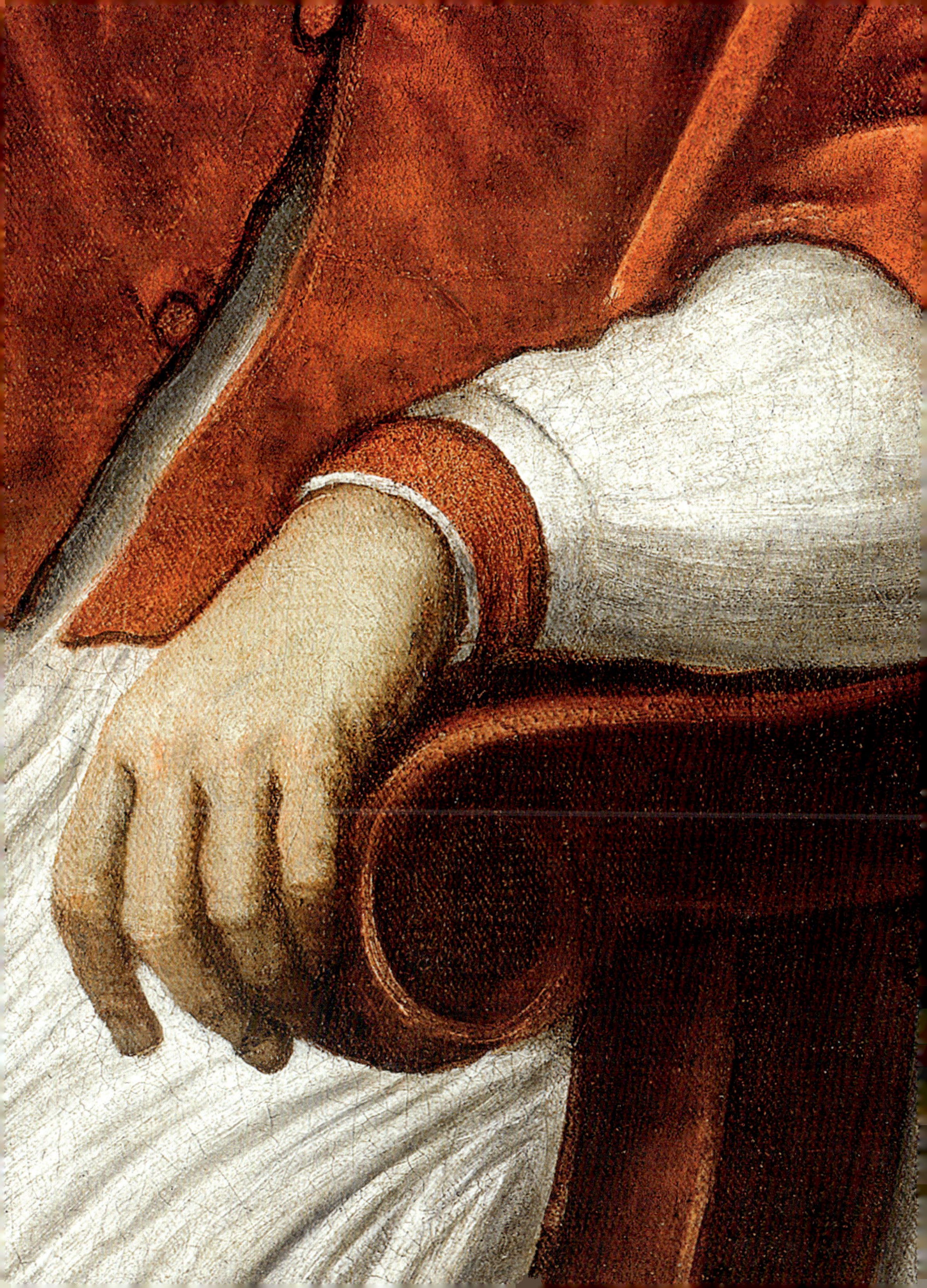

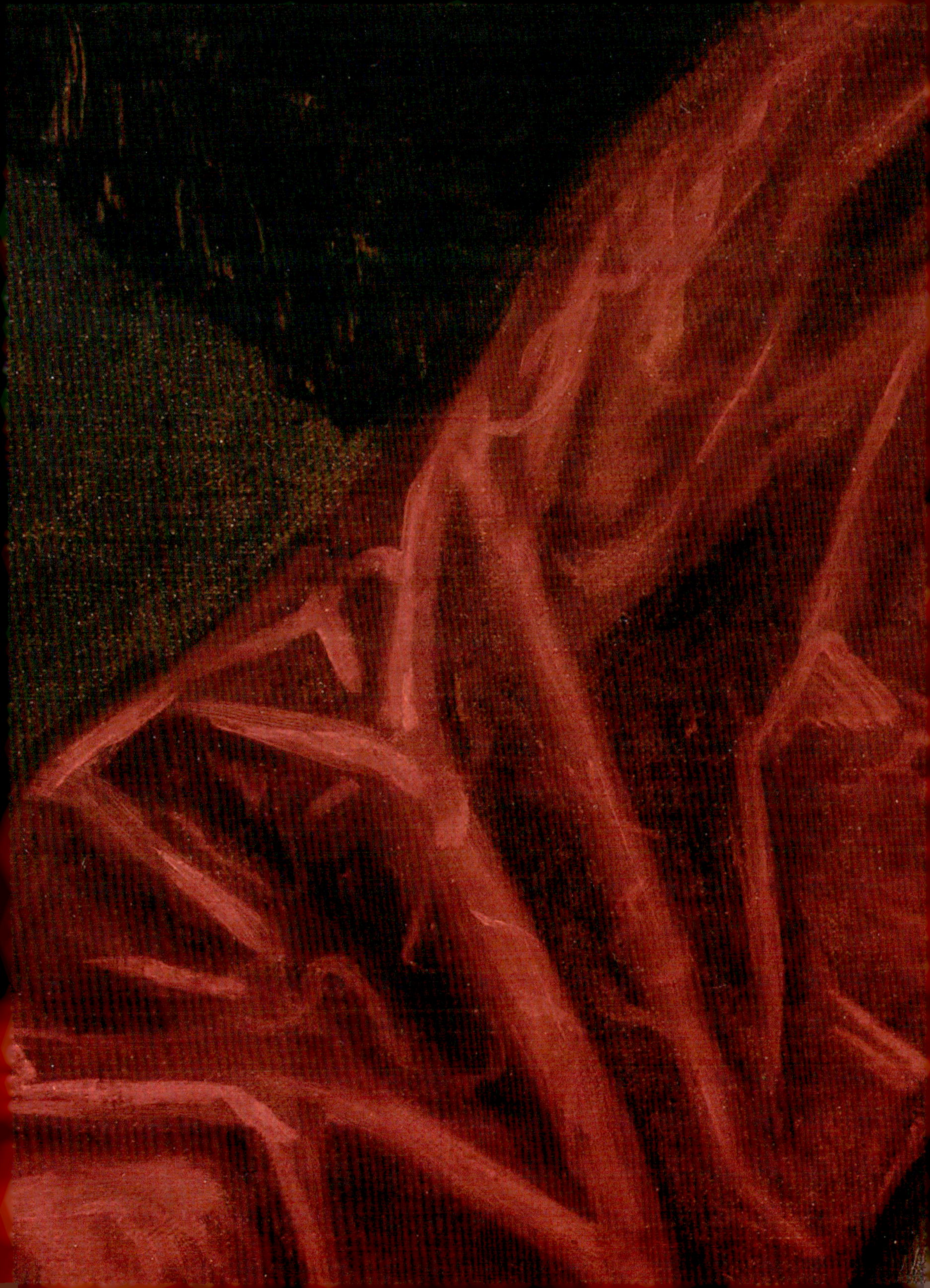

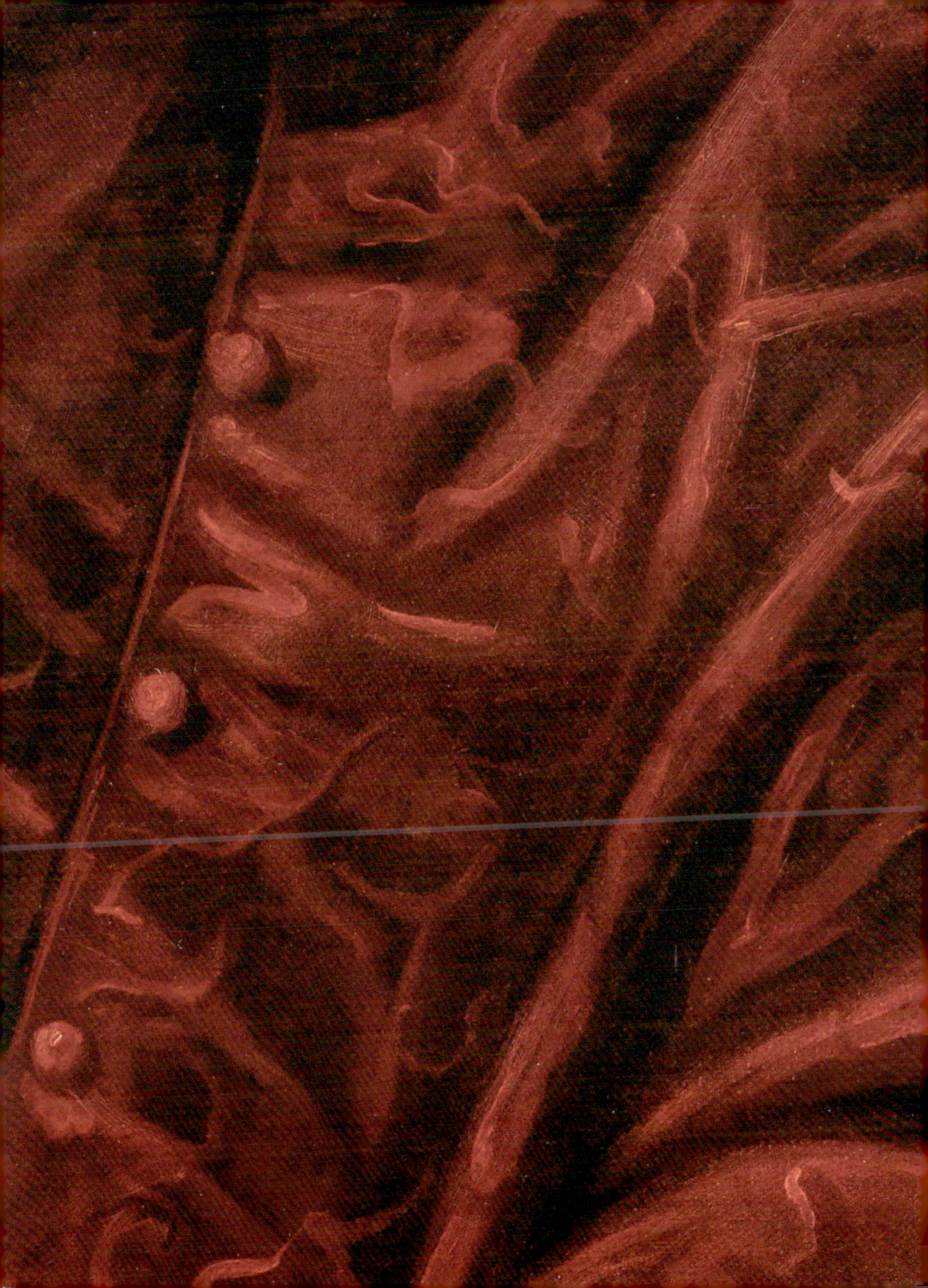

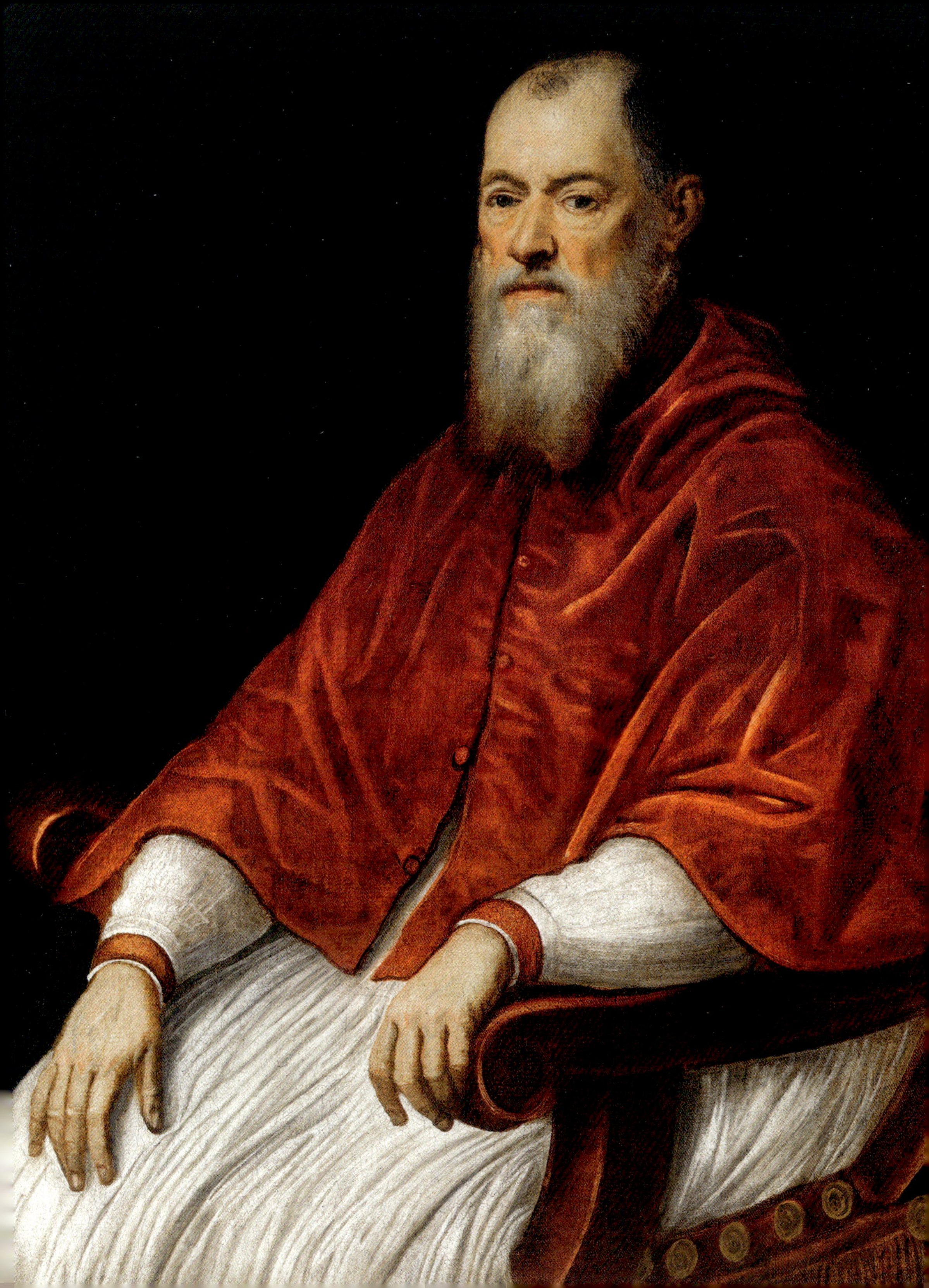

Tintoretto's portraits of Giovanni Grimani

Marsilio Arte

Tintoretto's portraits of Giovanni Grimani

Venice, Palazzo Grimani
17.04
—08.09.2024

Promoted by

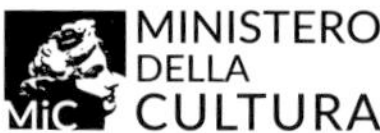

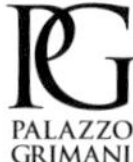

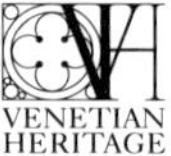

COLNAGHI
Est. 1760

Financed by
Venetian Heritage
Colnaghi

Exhibition curated by
Toto Bergamo Rossi
Daniele Ferrara
Valeria Finocchi

Organization of the exhibition, communication and Press Office
Valentina Farace
Valeria Finocchi
Marco Mazzocco

Administrative organization
Giorgio Ceccato
Bianca Restivo

Lenders
Colnaghi
Schorr Collection

Transport
Artèria

Insurance
Liberty

Lighting
Spazioluce

Graphic design
Livio Cassese

Printing of graphics in the exhibition
Gruppofallani

Exhibition texts
Valeria Finocchi
Marco Mazzocco

Catalogue texts
Daniele Ferrara
Valeria Finocchi
Giorgio Tagliaferro
Francesco Trentini

Translations
Gabriele Poole

Acknowledgements
Giulia Altissimo
Roberto Barison
Beverly Barkat
Andrea Bellieni
Martin Böhm
Annalisa Bristot
Sara Bolzicco
Gregorio Ceccon
Gemma Cortes
Cristina Crisafulli
Manuela Cuccuru
Matteo De Fina
Eliseba De Leonardis
Emma Dodd
Vania Gransinigh
Claire de la Haye
David Lewis
Howard Lewis
Carlo Alberto Manzan
Pepi Marchetti Franchi
Federica Mattiuzzo
Dania Nobile
Sabine Pichler-Koblinger
Mia Dora Pravan
Irene Spada
Devis Valenti
Nerea de Zabala

Daniele Ferrara
Director, Direzione regionale Musei Veneto

Valeria Finocchi
Director, Museo di Palazzo Grimani

The exhibition *Tintoretto's portraits of Giovanni Grimani* marks a new stage in the project of reconnecting Palazzo dei Grimani di Santa Maria Formosa to its history, its collections, and its role from the sixteenth century to the present. This project, characterized by a very effective public-private co-operation between the Direzione regionale Musei Veneto and Venetian Heritage, began in 2019 with the return of part of the original collection of antiquities to the "Tribuna" of Palazzo Grimani and continued with a reorganization of the Museo di Palazzo Grimani and a series of exhibition events aimed at promoting contemporary creativity, in line with the role of cultural laboratory that Palazzo has played since ancient times.

On this occasion, thanks to the crucial collaboration with Colnaghi, two important portraits of the patriarch Giovanni Grimani by Jacopo Tintoretto have been brought to the Museo di Palazzo Grimani, where they can now be compared with the portrait already in the Museum's collections, attributed to his son Domenico, acquired in 2020 thanks to Venetian Heritage's generous donation to the State. We therefore have the opportunity to update from an art-historical point of view our iconographic and iconological interpretation of these portraits and to further reflect on their attribution. Above all we have an opportunity to share this renewed debate with a wider public, to whom this catalog is addressed. We are delighted to have the possibility of working with Venetian Heritage on exhibition initiatives such as these: their temporary nature is not a limitation but a lasting investment in the public cultural heritage, permanently available to visitors, whose figurative and architectural expressions, along with the story of Giovanni Grimani's personal life, are a source of incredible interest and fascination.

Valentina Marini Clarelli Nasi

President, Fondazione Venetian Heritage Onlus, Venezia

Peter Marino

Chairman and President, Venetian Heritage Inc., New York

Since 1999, Venetian Heritage has been promoting Venetian culture through a vast campaign of restoration projects carried out not only in Venice but in all the territories that were once part of the Venetian Republic. This vast and ambitious program has received the support of Italian and international institutions, foundations, and patrons, united by the desire to preserve the incredible artistic heritage that the Venetian Republic disseminated in all the eastern Mediterranean from the Middle Ages to the end of the eighteenth century. Venetian Heritage continues to collect donations to help preserve and promote this cultural heritage, which is unique worldwide.

We are particularly proud to be able to present this catalog, published on the occasion of the exhibition *Tintoretto's portraits of Giovanni Grimani*, held at the Museo di Palazzo Grimani.

This volume is dedicated to the portraits of Giovanni Grimani, Patriarch of Aquileia, one of the most illustrious members of the Venetian patrician family, to whom we owe the current appearance of the palace of Santa Maria Formosa, dating to the sixteenth century, and the collection of statues recently returned to the palace, in the refurbished Tribuna and Sala del Doge.

The organization of the exhibition and the publication of the volume were possible thanks to the collaboration between the Direzione regionale Musei Veneto, Venetian Heritage, and Colnaghi Gallery.

Special thanks go to the authors of this volume, Daniele Ferrara, Valeria Finocchi, Giorgio Tagliaferro, and Francesco Trentini, whose studies have provided us with an updated reading of the depictions of the illustrious Patriarch of Aquileia.

We would also like to thank those who collaborated in the realization of the exhibition and the catalogue: Toto Bergamo Rossi, Livio Cassese, Jorge Coll, Gemma Cortes, Candida Lodovica de Angelis Corvi, Emma Dodd, Valentina Farace, Claire de la Haye, David Lewis, Howard Lewis, Marco Mazzocco, Gabriele Poole, Nerea de Zabala as well as all the firms that contributed to the realization of the exhibition.

Finally, we thank the office of Venetian Heritage for the dedication and care with which they carry out our activities.

Jorge Coll

Executive director, Colnaghi

Colnaghi's love affair with Venice began in 2019, when it staged a special exhibition—on the occasion of the Biennale—at the former Abbazia San Gregorio. Its aim was to attract global, contemporary connoisseurs, whose pursuit of aesthetic pleasure reflected that of eighteenth and nineteenth century Grand Tourists. In 2022, Colnaghi was also involved in Venetian Heritage's seminal exhibition of Renaissance sculptures at Galleria Giorgio Franchetti alla Ca' d'Oro, where our rediscovered terracotta bust by Donatello was one of the highlights.

Beyond recent history, however, Colnaghi has enjoyed strong links with Venice and Venetian painting for centuries. A masterpiece by Titian, the *Rape of Europa* (1559–1562), was acquired by Isabella Stewart Gardner through Colnaghi in 1896 and came to symbolise the extraordinary Old Masters acquisitions made by American collectors of the Gilded Age. Colnaghi's reputation for dealing museum-quality works was cemented, which heralded the establishment of a new tier in global collecting.

Colnaghi is, therefore, deeply honoured to be participating in a new Venetian project, a tribute to a leading political figure from the Republic of Venice in the sixteenth century: Giovanni Grimani. Hailing from a private collection, a striking portrait of Grimani was sold by Colnaghi in 1981(the same year, incidentally, in which David Bowie purchased *Angel Foretelling the Martyrdom of Saint Catherine of Alexandria* by Tintoretto—another key example of Venetian art collecting—from the gallery, later on loan at Palazzo Ducale).

More recently, Colnaghi rediscovered and sold Tintoretto's *Portrait of Tommaso Rangone.* It is only last year that, due to the London-based study of a privately-owned portrait depicting Giovanni Grimani, we realised that the attribution to the second portrait in this exhibition was correct.

I am deeply grateful to the Presidents and Board of Directors of Venetian Heritage (and hugely admiring, as ever, of the crucial and ambitious work they do to safeguard the heritage of the Republic of Venice), the Direzione regionale Musei Veneto and the Museo di Palazzo Grimani, the Lewis family, the Colnaghi Foundation and all the institutional and individual partners who contributed to the ideation and creation of this project.

Toto Bergamo Rossi

Director, Fondazione Venetian Heritage Onlus

Venetian Heritage is an international nonprofit organization that for twenty-five years supported cultural projects through conservation, exhibitions, publications, conferences, academic study, and research. The organization aims to increase awareness of the immense legacy of Venetian art in Italy and in those areas once part of the Republic of Venice.

One of the most important projects supported in Venice, to cite only a few, has been the cleaning of the façades of the church of Gesuiti and the church of San Zaccaria, one of the finest examples of early Venetian Renaissance architecture. Venetian Heritage has also financed the restoration of the monumental staircase built by Mauro Codussi in 1498 in the Scuola Grande San Giovanni Evangelista.

Thanks to a fruitful collaboration with the Gallerie dell'Accademia, Venetian Heritage has financed the permanent installation in the first six rooms of the museum's new ground floor exhibition spaces and the restoration of several masterpieces, including *Il Castigo dei Serpenti* by Giambattista Tiepolo.

In Padua, Venetian Heritage has funded the restoration of the famous chapel of Saint Anthony in the Basilica of that same name.

The organization has also supported the training of specialized restorers. In Croatia, Venetian Heritage has financed the restoration of the façade of the Trogir Cathedral and the Orsini Chapel. In cooperation with several co-donors, Venetian Heritage has financed the restoration of the magnificent façade of the Cathedral of Saint Mark on Korcula, a Dalmatian Island that was part of the Republic of Venice from 1200 to the fall of the Serenissima in 1797.

In the past decade, Venetian Heritage has expanded its reach through a series of interventions designed not only to preserve important masterpieces of Venetian art but also to support and expand a number of Venetian National museums, with projects such as the renovation of the Palazzo Grimani museum, with the return of the original sculpture collection to the palace after 400 years, and the ongoing restoration and restyling of the Galleria Giorgio Franchetti alla Ca' d'Oro, where Venetian Heritage has also organized and financed the exhibition *From Donatello To Alessandro Vittoria 1450–1600, 150 Years of Sculpture in the Republic of Venice.*

The exhibition *Tintoretto's portraits of Giovanni Grimani* is part of the path of promotion of the history and collections of the Museo di Palazzo Grimani begun in 2019 with the reinstallation of the collection of classical statues in the Tribuna Grimani and the Sala del Doge, carried out thanks to a very effective collaboration between the Direzione regionale Musei Veneto and Venetian Heritage.

In 2020, thanks to a referral from the Milan Export Office of the Italian Ministry of Culture, Venetian Heritage was able to acquire and donate to the museum a *Portrait of Patriarch Giovanni Grimani* attributed to Domenico Tintoretto dated to the early seventeenth century. The presence of this work of art in Palazzo Grimani filled an important iconographic void, as the portrait of the *parón de casa* to whom the building owes its current aspect, unique in Venice because of its architectural conformation reminiscent of a Roman domus, inspired by the great buildings of the papal city.

The exhibition allows us to compare the portrait made by Domenico Tintoretto with two paintings by his father Jacopo Tintoretto. An exceptional loan is a small oil on panel painting depicting the *Portrait of Giovanni Grimani*, recently rediscovered in a private collection by the Colnaghi Gallery and shown to the public for the first time in this exhibition. The panel was made by Jacopo Tintoretto probably as a model for the execution of two of the artist's masterpieces: the *Portrait of Giovanni Grimani* belonging to the Schorr Collection, also on display in the exhibition, and the well-known *Portrait of Giovanni Grimani* in the Rijksmuseum in Amsterdam.

Colnaghi with the Direzione regionale Musei Veneto and Venetian Heritage promotes and supports this exhibition project. The operation represents yet another virtuous example of public-private collaboration, and it is my greatest hope that one day the panel painting depicting Giovanni Grimani will join the collections of the Museo di Palazzo Grimani.

Cover
Jacopo Tintoretto,
Portrait of Giovanni Grimani,
second half of the sixteenth century
Private collection

Design and layout
Livio Cassese

©2024 by Marsilio Arte s.r.l.

First edition April 2024

ISBN 979-12-546-3237-6

Reproduction and printing by
Grafiche Veneziane s.c.r.l., Venice
for Marsilio Editori® s.p.a., Venice

contents

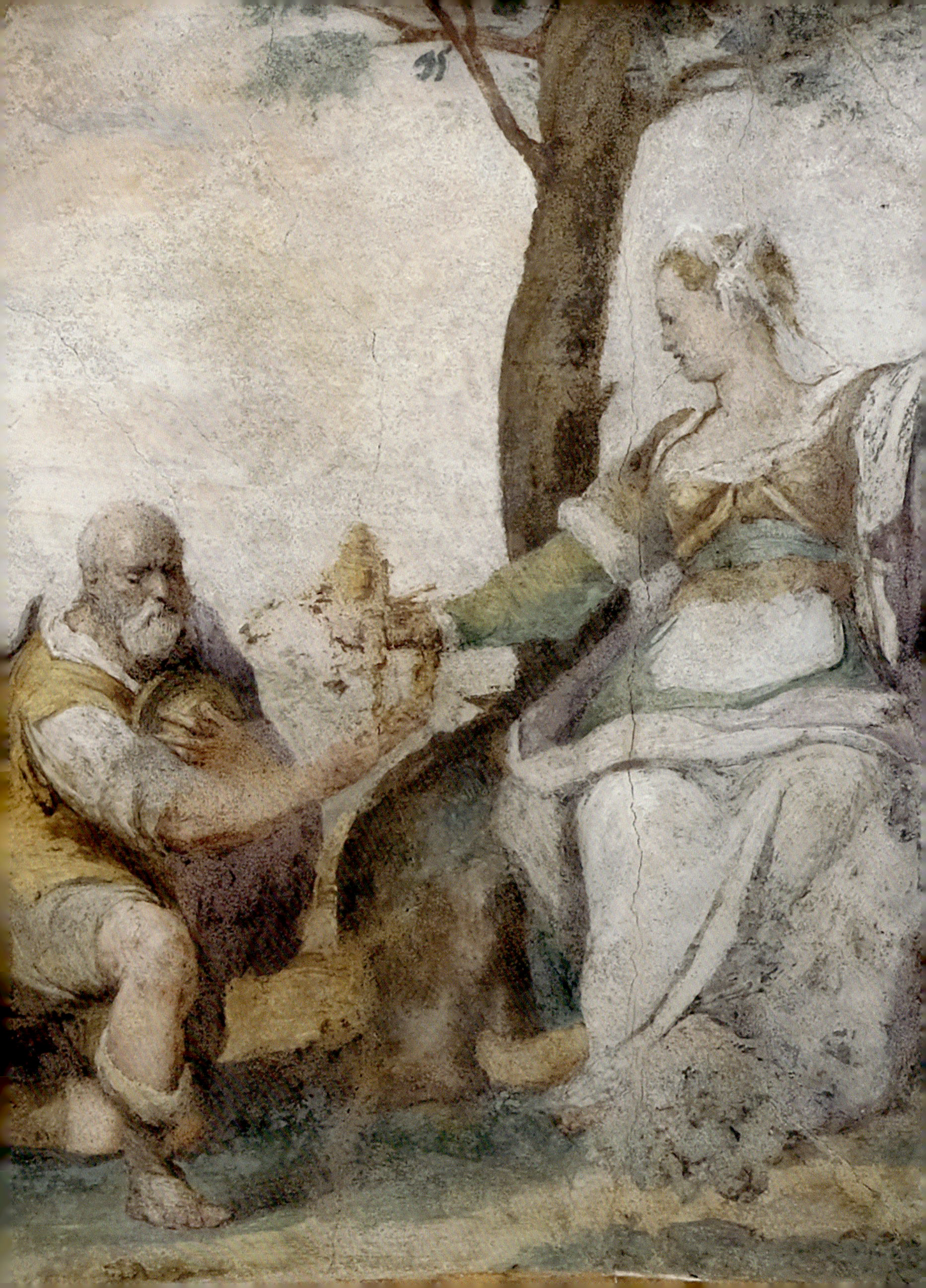

Iconography of Giovanni Grimani: objects, sources, open issues

Daniele Ferrara, Valeria Finocchi[1]

Between biography and iconography

In a fundamental and still highly relevant essay on the theory and history of Venetian portrait painting in the sixteenth century, art historian Enrico Castelnuovo illustrates what was to become one of the distinctive features of the genre, following a path opened by Titian Vecellio (who continued and innovated Raphael's teachings) and pursued by other painters, such as Jacopo Tintoretto himself. This specific feature can be described as the ability,

to envelop a character in a symbolic aura, discretely evoked by attributes, tools, objects laden with allusions, to present him in such a way that his image occupies entirely the field of allegorical and super-individual meanings one wishes to attribute to it, but in such a way that at the same time it does not seem in any way depersonalized, so that it can be read *as a metaphor and as a story*.[2]

The exhibition that this volume accompanies intends precisely to investigate, through the examination of three of the many portraits of Patriarch Giovanni Grimani, the ways in which the image of the Venetian prelate has been defined through the medium of painting along two lines: that of the *meanings*, also allegorical, that his effigies convey, and that of Grimani's actual physical aspect as depicted over time, keeping in mind that the purpose of the portraits was also to perpetuate the memory of this illustrious figure, so that it could serve as an example for posterity, and the strategy adopted was that of establishing a recognizable physiognomy and highlighting the values associated with the figure.

It was perhaps this desire that led an other Giovanni Grimani, this one of the San Boldo branch, to commission the manuscript preserved in the Correr Museum Library in Venice, entitled *Origine della famiglia Grimana*.[3] The volume presents a succession of biographical profiles of the main members of this old and most prestigious lineage of the Venetian Serenissima. The subjects belonged to various branches of the family, starting with the founder, Grimoaldo King of Apulia, who lived in the seventh century, up to Antonio of the branch of Santa Maria Formosa, bishop of Torcello, who lived at the turn of the sixteenth century.[4] The manuscript is dated 1627 on the frontispiece,[5] but it is in fact unfinished. Each text, of varying length, is always accompanied by a half-length portrait drawn in pen and sometimes by other figurative elements such as medals, coins, coats of arms and emblems.

The drawings, characterized by a certain liveliness, are not meant as a mere companion to the text, which is often limited to a handful of lines, having instead the place of honor within the page. The most important members of the branch of Santa Maria Formosa, including the ones responsible for originally purchasing and renovating the palace are all present. Among the latter, the first is Antonio (1435–1523), founder of the family branch, a successful merchant and also doge late in life; his son Domenico (1461–1523), a fine theologian, a powerful cardinal in Rome and the first member of the branch to hold the title of Patriarch of Aquileia; Domenico's brother, Gerolamo (1466–1515), father in turn of four brothers who were all important in the family history of the sixteenth century, namely Cardinal Marino (1488/89–1546), the procurator and later patriarch Marco (1494–1544), the procurator of San Marco, Vettore (1495–1558), and finally the protagonist of this exhibition, the antiquities collector and patriarch of Aquileia, Giovanni Grimani.

The page assigned in the manuscript to the biography of Giovanni Grimani (fig. 1) shows at the top a half-length portrait accompanied by some attributes that emphasize his status as patriarch and patron, while at the bottom of the text are shown the two sides of a medal the *recto* shows the profile portrait of the prelate and closely resembles two other identi-

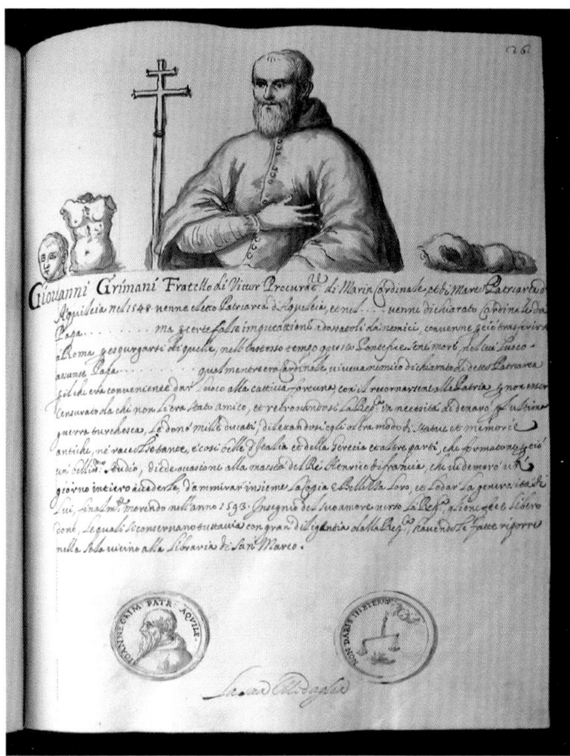

1

Portrait of Giovanni Grimani excerpt from *Origine della famiglia Grimana*, 1627, MS. 270, fondo Morosini-Grimani, Venice, Library of Museo Correr

cal specimens preserved in the numismatic collections of the Museo Correr, while in a third medal, preserved at the Musei Civici di Udine, Giovanni Grimani is depicted with more synthetic physiognomic traits, but still substantially identifiable.[6] The reverse of the medal depicted on the page of the Correr Manuscript (unfortunately, no known specimens of this are preserved) features the inscription IOANNE GRI: PATR: AQUILE and an emblem with scales, fire and a putto in the act of blowing, accompanied by the motto "Non dabis in eternum," the same found in one of the lunettes of the *Sala a Fogliami* in Palazzo Grimani (fig. 2). The effigy, attributes, and allegorical elements all contain references to the life and interests of the Giovanni, contributing to the effective overall interaction of text and image.

In the following pages, we will seek to reconstruct the iconographic path that led to the definition of this recognizable image of Giovanni Grimani, a path that is not linear and that presents some critical hurdles, discussed in the in-depth studies by Daniele Ferrara, Francesco Trentini and Giorgio

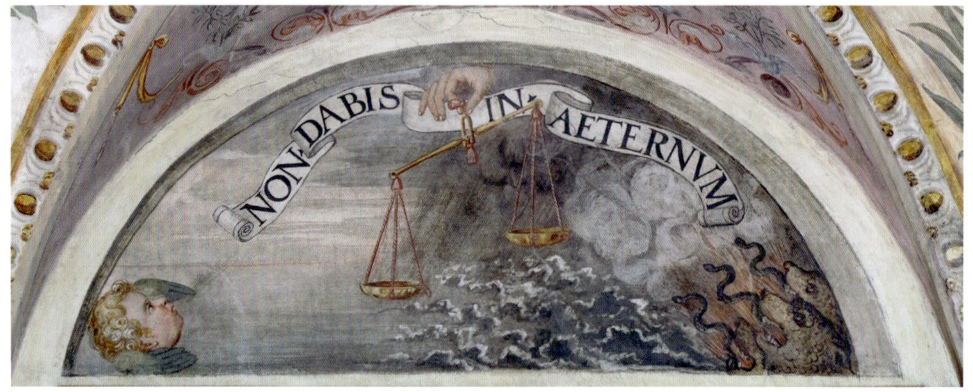

2
Lunette in the *Sala a Fogliami,*
Museo di Palazzo Grimani

Tagliaferro. It is therefore worthwhile, before reviewing these effigies, to briefly retrace the main stages in the life of this central figure of sixteenth century Venice.[7]

Born probably in 1506, Giovanni Grimani was destined early on for an ecclesiastical career like his older brother Marino. He held the office of bishop of Ceneda and commendatory of the Abbey of Santa Maria di Sesto al Reghena and, in two different periods of his life (from 1545 to 1550 and from 1585 to his death in 1593), of patriarch of Aquileia, a title that remained in the the Grimani family, with few interruptions, from the end of the fifteenth century until the beginning of the seventeenth century. But Giovanni was above all a passionate and knowledgeable patron and collector, active particularly in the Venetian Republic (including the Venetian and Friulian territories) and in Rome, where the Grimani owned a piece of land—the famous Vigna—on the Quirinal Hill. These two territories where also the two main centers on which the family, which belonged to the "papalist" faction of the Venetian patriciate, based its political and cultural power.[8] Early on, Giovanni had been called upon to bolster this power also by pursuing an ecclesiastical career that was meant to lead him, like the other family prelates, to the position of cardinal. This position, however, was ultimately denied to him, due to an accusation of heresy for

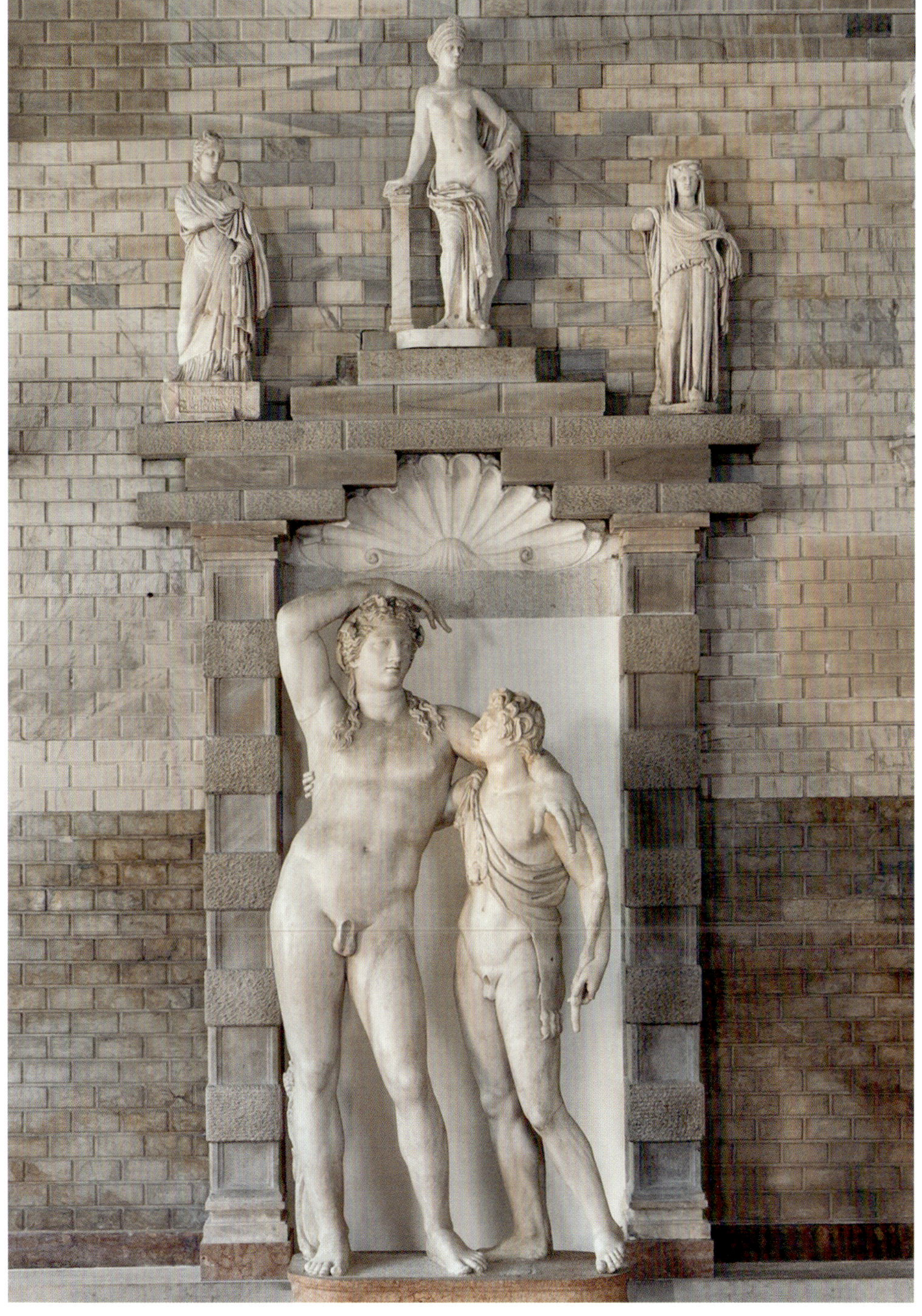

3
The *Sala del Doge*,
Museo di Palazzo Grimani

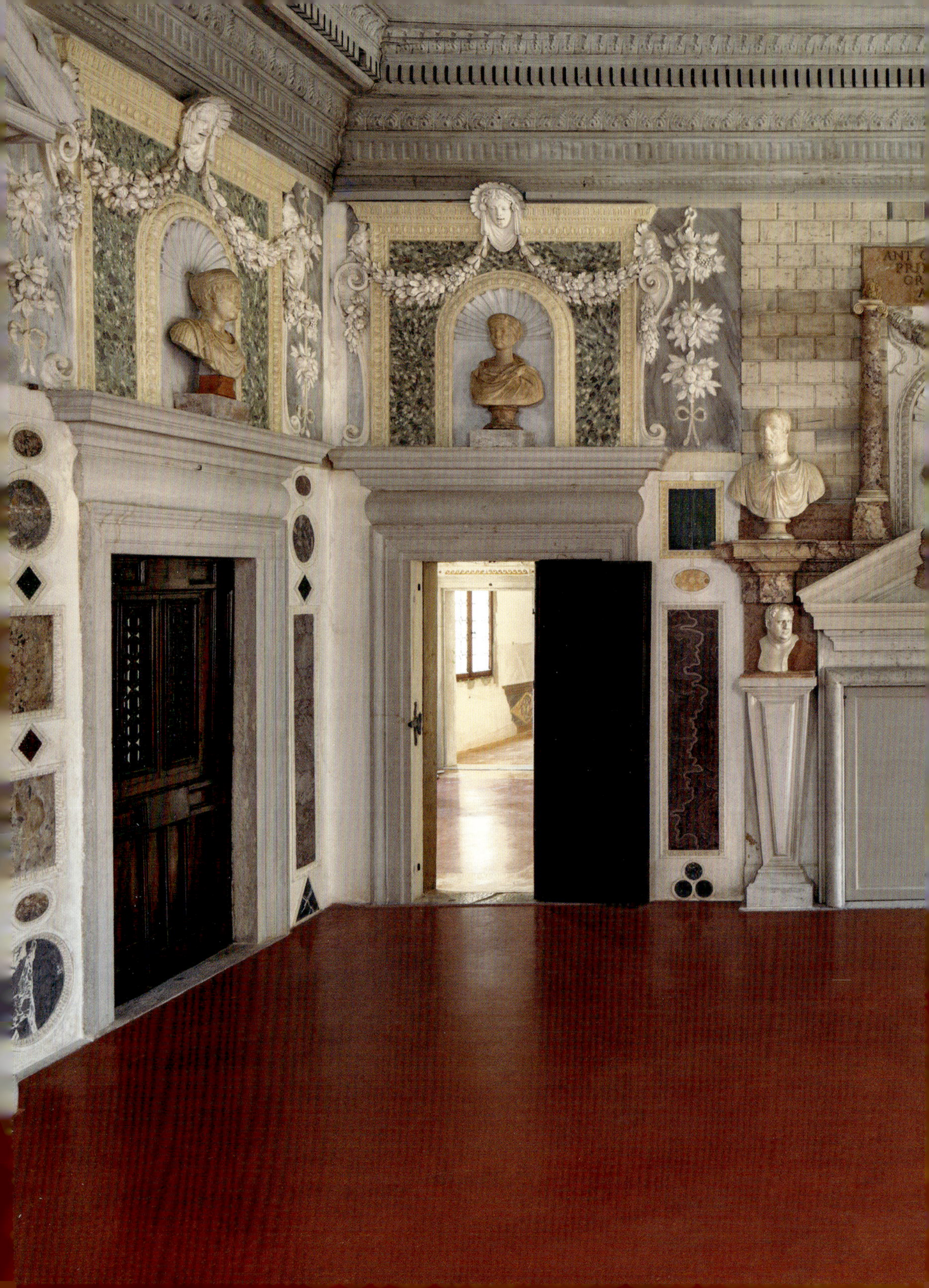
ANT
PR
GR
A

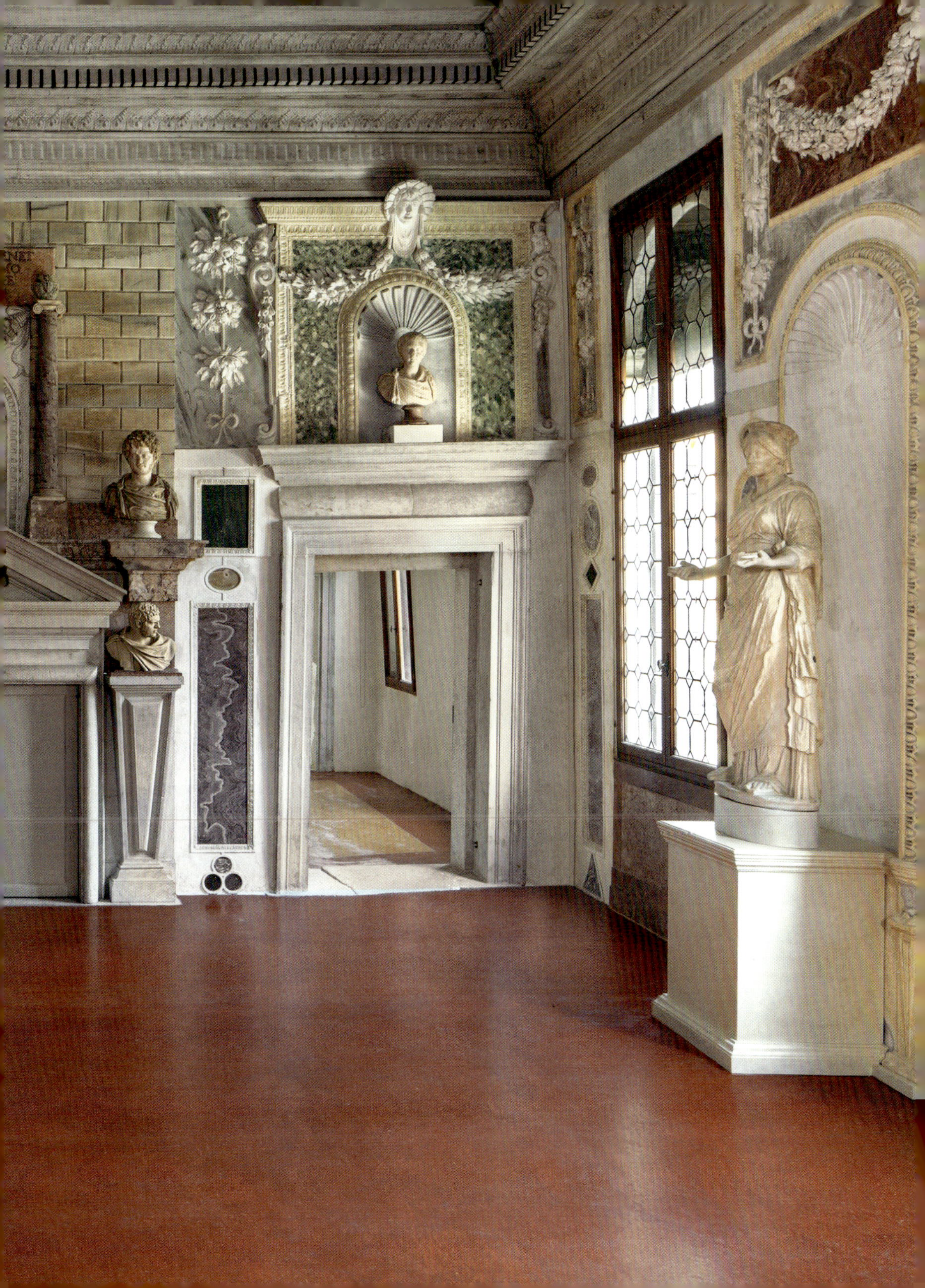

a suspected sympathy for Lutheran ideas, from which he was eventually absolved, but which remained as an indelible stain on his reputation, so that no pontiff ever agreed to bestow on him the title.[9]

Giovanni Grimani favored Greek and Roman antiquities, like his uncle Domenico before him, which he collected throughout his life, accumulating a considerable number of sculptures, architectural fragments, epigraphs but also cameos, coins and medals. Giovanni did not limit himself to this: after remaining the sole owner of the palace in Santa Maria Formosa (his brothers Marino and Marco passed first, followed by his brother Vettore in 1558, leaving no heirs), Giovanni carried out an old family project, doubling the size of the building, which had been purchased in the second half of the fifteenth century by his grandfather Antonio, and adding to its typically Venetian and medieval aspect a distinct Roman flair (the models for which were the *domus antica* and the coeval palaces of Rome, such as Palazzo Farnese or Palazzo Altemps). The success of the project was insured by Giovanni's passion and skill as an "amateur" of architecture[10] and by his ties with the leading architects of the time, including Jacopo Sansovino, Sebastiano Serlio, Andrea Palladio, and Vincenzo Scamozzi. "Roman" classical elements were in fact already found on some of the ceilings of the oldest rooms, the mythological *camerini*, where Giovanni and Vettore, between 1539 and 1542, had employed artists with a Tuscan-Roman background, such as Giovanni da Udine and Francesco Salviati,[11] to work on stucco and frescoes. Following the enlargement of the building, other painters, once again of non-Venetian extraction, were called upon to decorate the new rooms, namely the "Mantuan", Camillo Capelli, author of the luxuriant ceiling of the *Sala a Fogliami*,[12] and a young Federico Zuccari, who was responsible the scenes in the sophisticated vault of the monumental staircase.[13]

Patriarch Giovanni's personal choices left their mark also on the destination of the rooms, especially the *Piano Nobile*. It was here that he placed many of his sculptures and antiquities, all closely coordinated with the decorations in order to create allegorical itineraries of neo-Platonic inspiration, though within a Christian perspective. Giovanni also had two other rooms prepared in which the sculpture were integrated with architecture: the *Sala del Doge* (fig. 3), dedicated to the memory of his grandfather Antonio, and above all

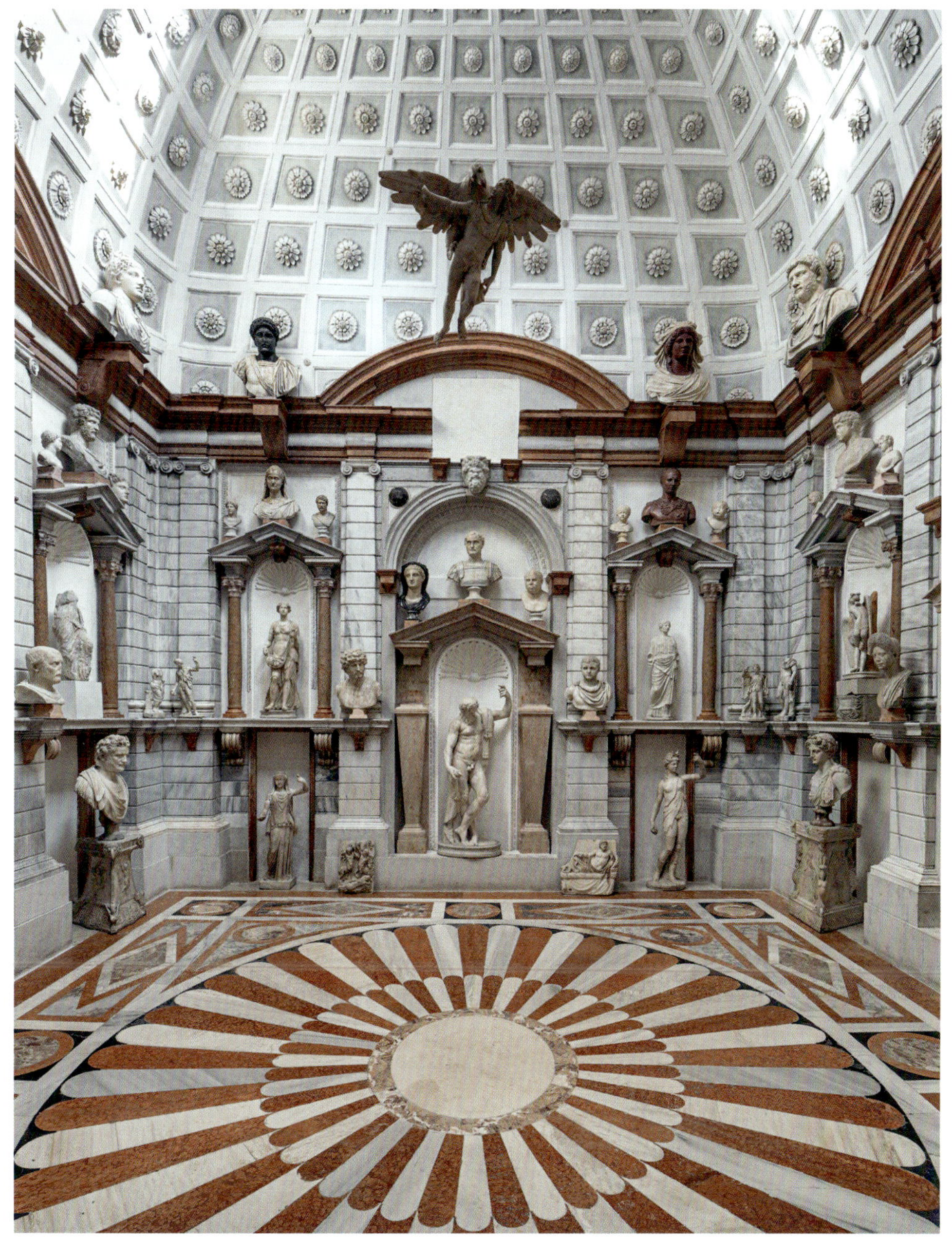

4
The *Tribuna*,
Museo di Palazzo Grimani

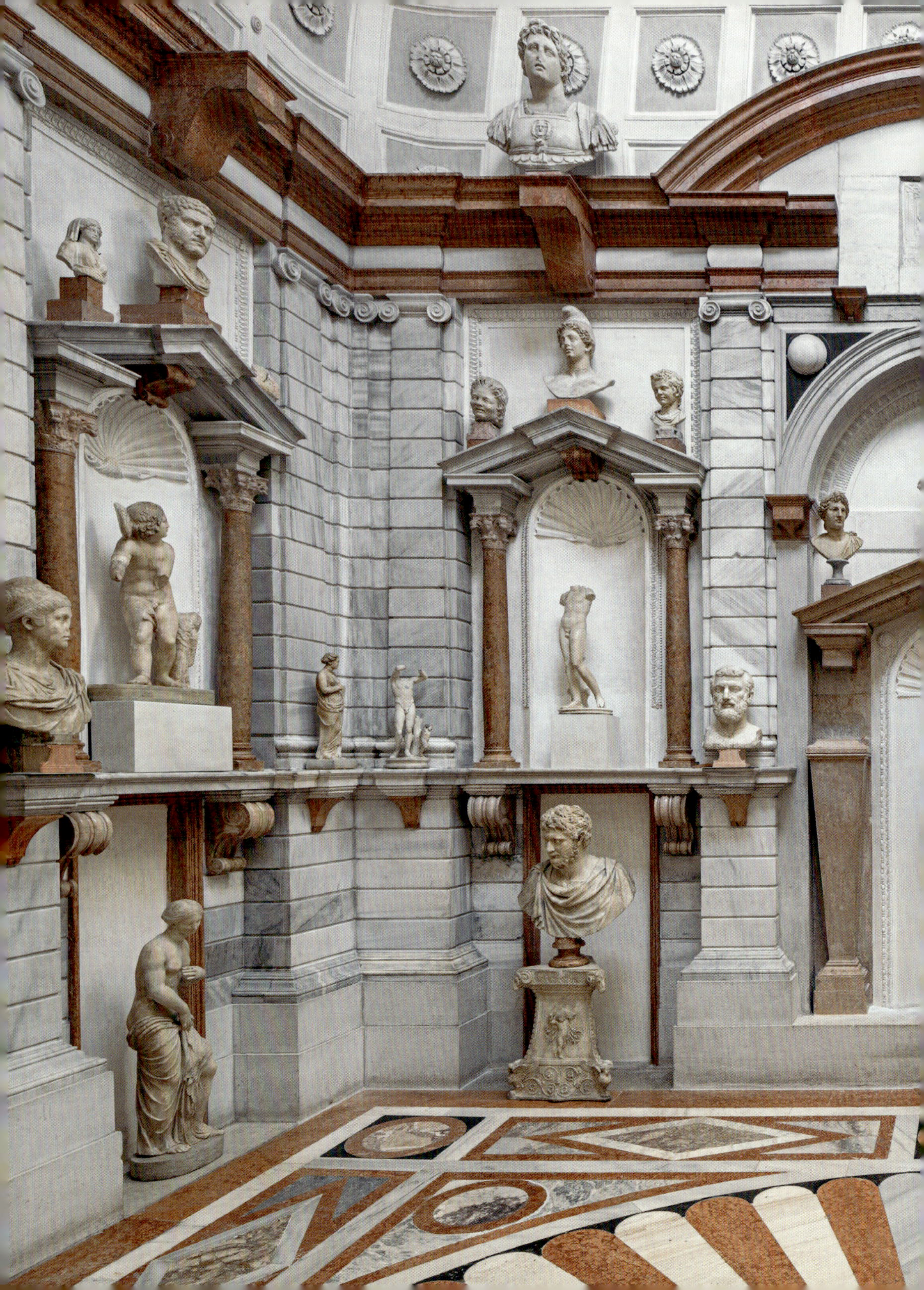

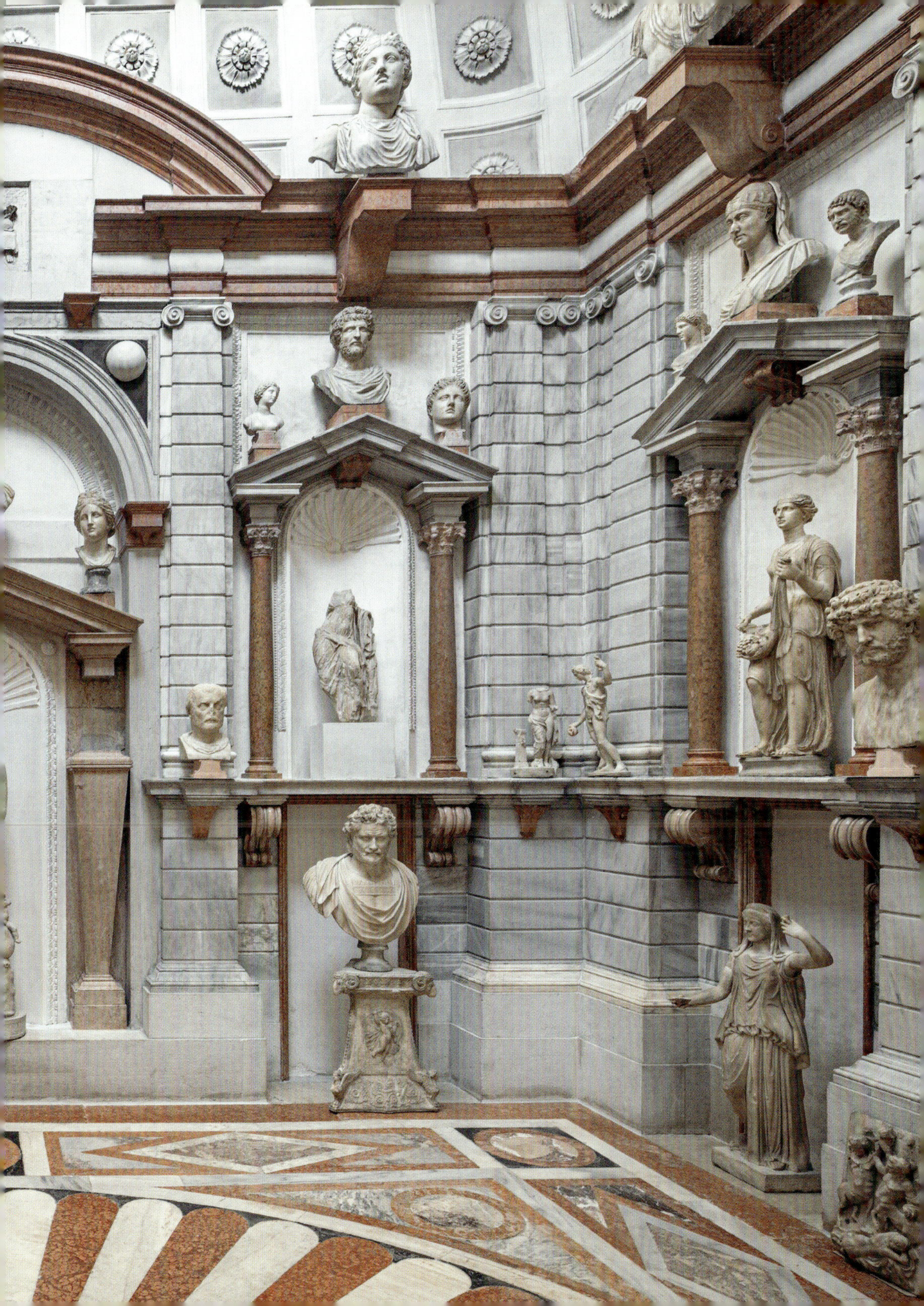

the famous chamber of antiquities, now known as the *Tribuna* (fig. 4), a specifically museum-like space intended to house the most conspicuous and most valuable part of the collection, in which Giovanni, following Sebastiano Serlio's recommendation, had a skylight installed to provide better lighting for the antiquities.[14] The result made the palace a wonder, a *unicum* not only in Venice but in all Europe, attracting illustrious guests that included humanists, philosophers, religious authorities and noblemen, including the King of France Henry III, who were welcomed and accompanied on their visit and entertained with lavish banquets and musical performances.

In 1587, Giovanni Grimani donated to the Republic his prestigious collection (the donation was finalised in 1594, after his death the previous year), which was transferred to a Statuary located the Anteroom of the Libreria Marciana, based on a project by Vincenzo Scamozzi supervised by Grimani himself. The Statuary was renovated over the centuries and was the core of the Museo Archeologico Nazionale di Venezia.[15] Today, part of the collection has been returned the rooms of the Palazzo di Santa Maria Formosa and especially to the *Tribuna*, thanks to a project carried out in collaboration with the Venetian Heritage Foundation in 2019 and 2021.[16]

Portraits of Giovanni Grimani

Giovanni Grimani appears in numerous portraits that are characterized by a certain typological variety and are difficult to place in a precise chronological sequence. We already mentioned the portrait in the Correr manuscript, to which we can associate the profile of the medal shown on the page with those of the other two known types of medals. Here Giovanni is depicted with a characteristic medium-length beard, a receding hairline on the head and not too advanced in age. This portrait belongs to a group of many portraits of Giovanni, almost all of which have already been the subject of analysis and interpretation.[17]

We refer first of all to portraits painted on panel or canvas, starting with the one that has now become part of the collections of the Museo di Palazzo Grimani.[18] In some of these, only the face and shoulders are visible. This is the case of the small-format canvas (61.5 × 47 cm) in the Rijksmuseum in

Amsterdam attributed to Jacopo Tintoretto (cf. p, 80),[19] which shows the patriarch Grimani in his mature years, and is datable between the 1650s and 1660s.[20] The prelate is wearing his as usual the *mozzetta*, a short-hooded cape, which here appears to be of a dark red color, somewhere between cardinal purple and bishop violet. This, however, could be the result of the darkening of the paint. Giovanni has a calm and profound gaze, suggesting a man devoted to reflection and contemplation.

Another portrait (oil on canvas, 57×49.5 cm) of similar format and size was auctioned by Sotheby's (cf. p. 67) in 2004 and belongs now to Soumaya Museum in Mexico City. It is similar in terms of the expression, with a few differences in the facial expression (the left corner of the mouth seems to curve into a hint of a smile) and in some physiognomic features. Giovanni here appears much older than in the previous painting: his hairline more receding, his beard and hair completely white and the *mozzetta* is a bright red damask. The age and clothing suggest that the work was made toward the end of the prelate's life, in the 1680s, as Francesco Trentini states in the catalog. The attribution of the painting to Jacopo Tintoretto, with Domenico, is not fully convincing.

From these two paintings derive further versions, with a similar depiction of the visage, belonging to the subgenre of the *state portrait*.[21] These include the small panel (57.5×40.5 cm) from a private collection displayed in the exhibition (cf. p. 75) and first published in 1927 by Adolfo Venturi,[22] where Giovanni appears once again dressed as a prelate, with the *mozzetta* and here also the white *rocchetto* (the robe) underneath. He is showed in a three-quarter view, seated on a pew, while behind him a dark curtain can be glimpsed, and the figure is cut off at the level of the hands. The portrait was actually a study for a larger painting, which has been identified as the portrait (oil on canvas, 115×102 cm) formerly in the Vivian-Neal collection and now belonging to the Schorr collection (cf. p. 77), from which it has arrived at Palazzo Grimani on the occasion of the exhibition.[23] Rodolfo Pallucchini has reconstructed, in a fundamental essay published in *Arte Veneta* in 1983, the collection history of the canvas: the work was purchased by the English nobleman George Vivian in 1828 directly from Michele Grimani, the last descendant of the branch of Santa Maria Formosa, intent in those years on

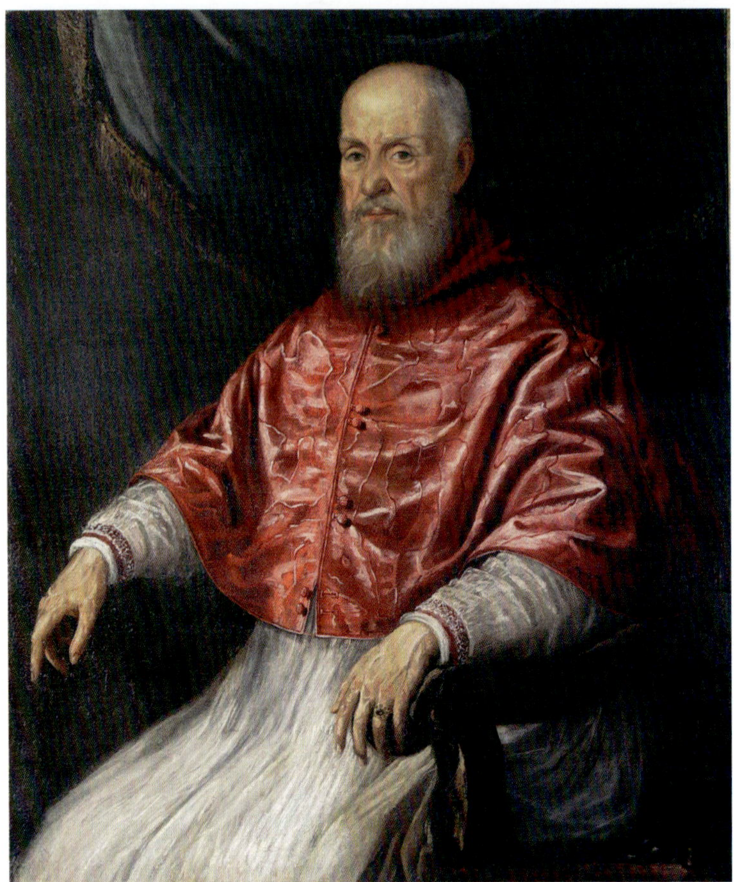

5
Author unknown, *Portrait of
Giovanni Grimani*, second half
of the sixteenth century
oil on canvas, 111 × 91.5 cm
Private collection

placing pieces from the family collections still in the Palazzo on the market
for economic reason but probably also because of his lack of interest in
art objects.[24] After several changes in ownership, it was sold in London at
Christie's on December 12, 1980, and then came into the Schorr collection.

Pallucchini hypothesizes for this canvas too the hand of Jacopo
Tintoretto dating it around 1560. Giovanni is portrayed in a manner entirely identical to the private collection panel, but the figure is cut off at
knee height, allowing us to fully appreciate the position of the hands, the
right resting on the armrest, the left lying on the robe that shows no trace

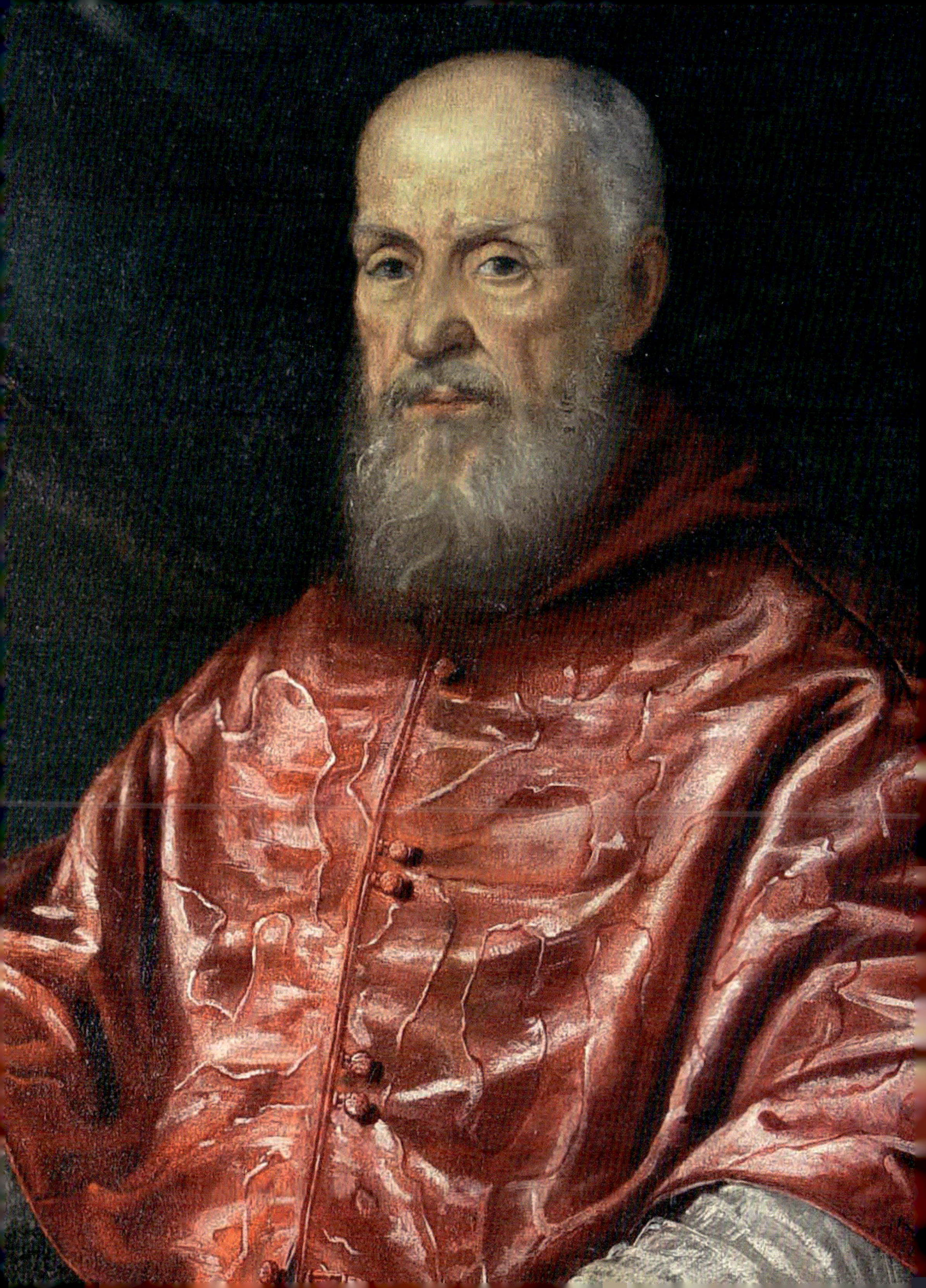

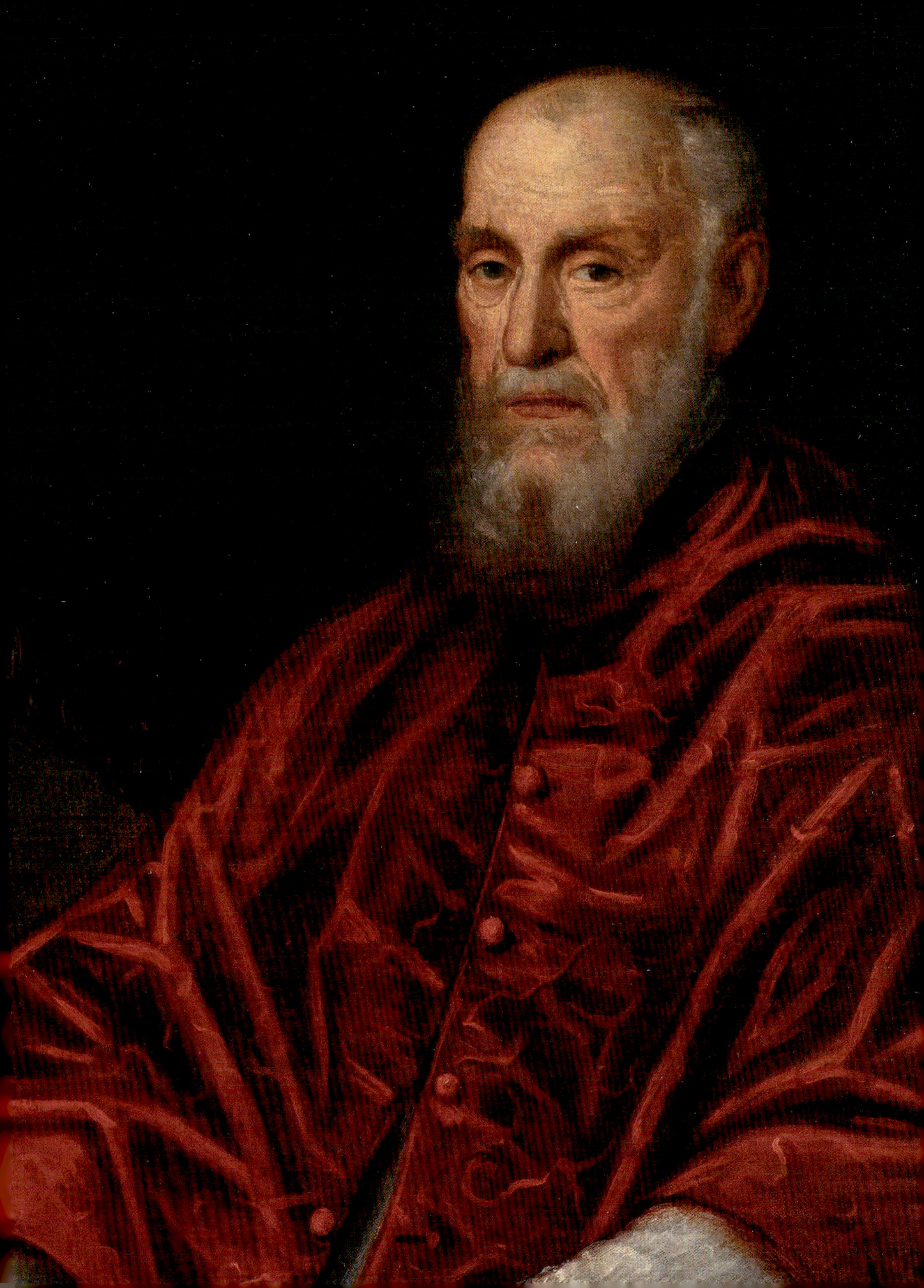

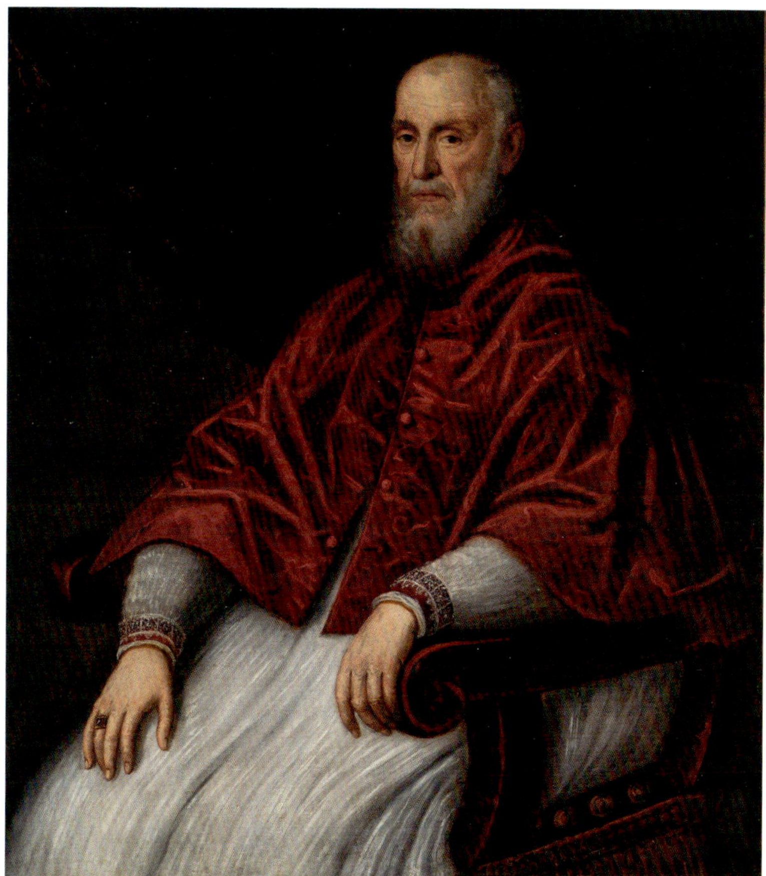

6
Domenico Tintoretto (attr.), *Portrait
of Giovanni Grimani*, end of sixteenth
– beginning of seventeenth century
oil on canvas, 116 × 101 cm
Museo di Palazzo Grimani

of decoration, just as there are no attributes present that would allow us to confirm the identification or recall, for example, the Patriarch's collecting passion. It is with all evidence an official portrait in which maximum emphasis is given solely to Grimani's position, more than his individuality.

The same compositional scheme is found in two other paintings, in which however the physiognomy recalls that of the above-mentioned portrait in Soumaya Museum. Both paintings show Giovanni Grimani again in old age, seated on a stool, the figure framed by the fringed curtain in the background, but certain differences are evident. The first of the two (oil on canvas, 111 × 91.5 cm; fig. 5) was published in 1969[25] by Pallucchini as a *Portrait of*

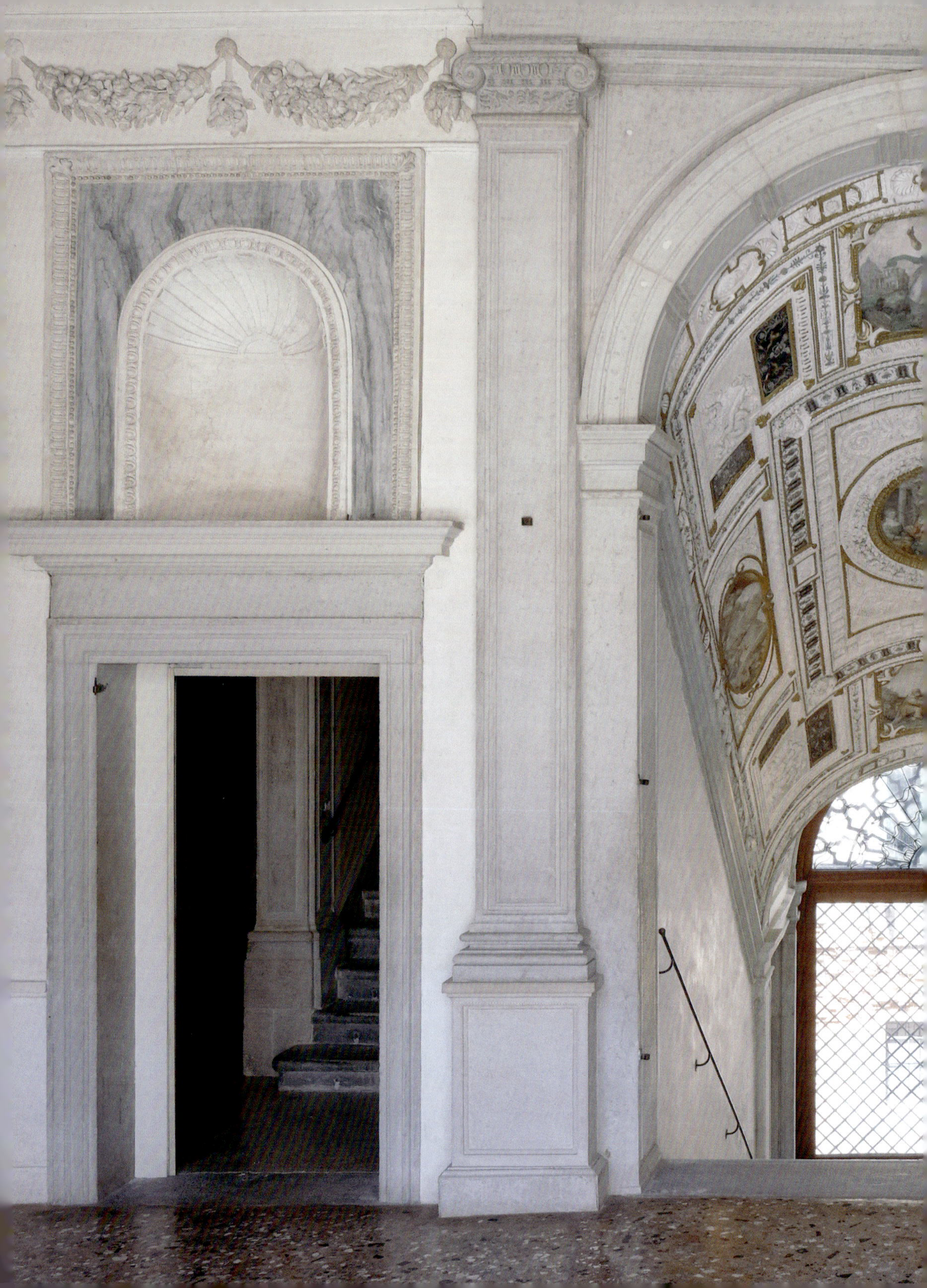

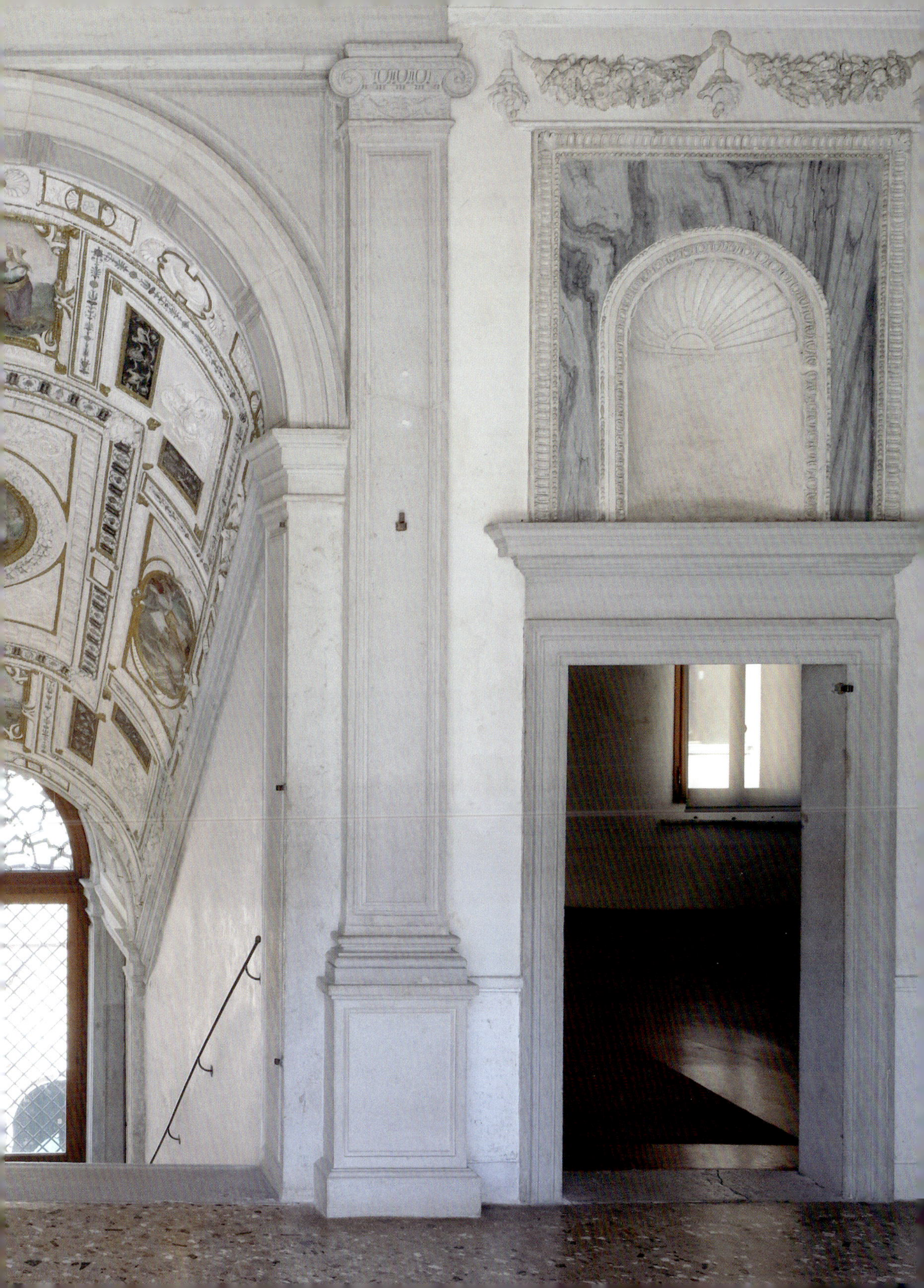

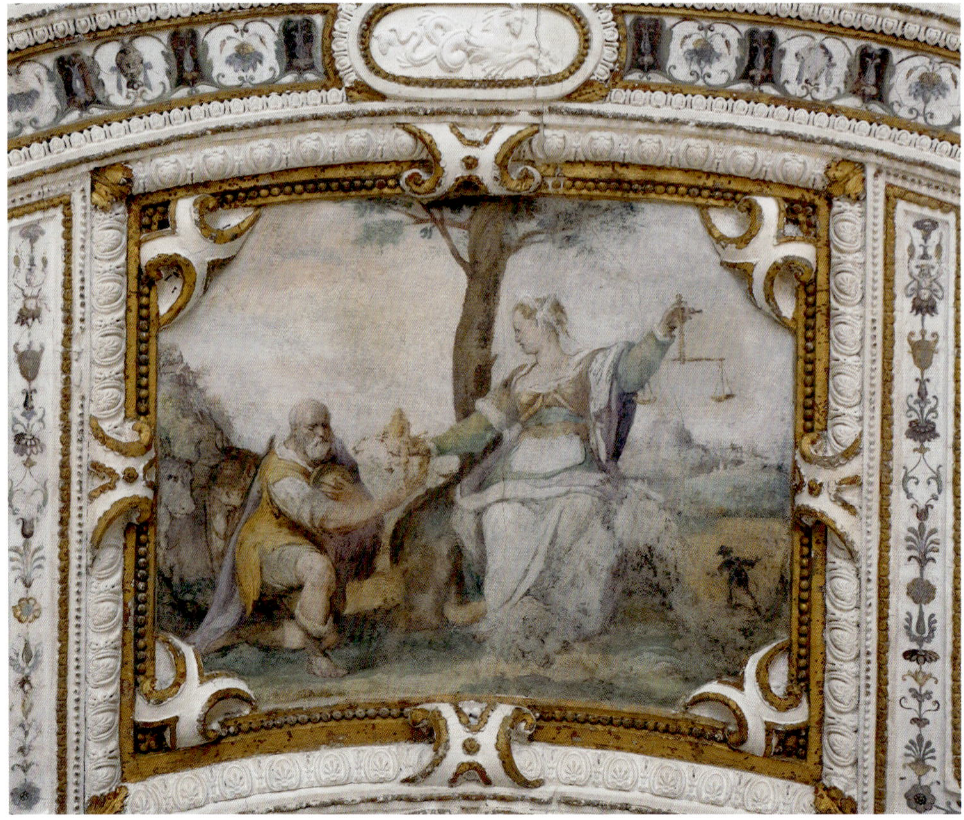

7
Federico Zuccari, *Distributive Justice*,
ca. 1565
Monumental Staircase,
Museo di Palazzo Grimani

Pietro Bembo and, more recently,[26] by Lionello Puppi, who correctly identifies the subject as Giovanni Grimani; it is kept in a private collection. Puppi proposes an attribution Domínikos Theotocópoulos, better known as El Greco, the amous artist of the Titian circle, who could have executed the painting "soon after his return to Venice around 1573."[27] Some slight but substantial compositional differences from the Schorr canvas are immediately apparent, such as the position of the right arm, with the hand resting on the armrest instead of on the lap, the embroidery of the cuffs, again the damask treatment of the *mozzetta*, and especially the presence of a ring on the left ring finger.

The second of the two portraits (oil on canvas, 116 × 101 cm) is the one now in the Museo di Palazzo Grimani (fig. 6). Here too Giovanni's facial features and tired expression suggest an extremely advanced age and therefore

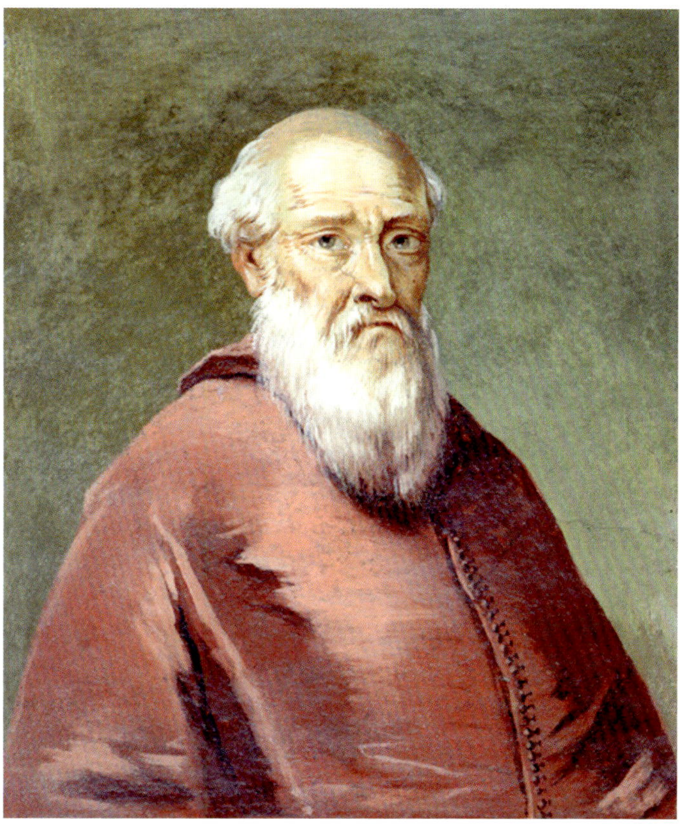

8
Author unknown, *Portrait of Giovanni Grimani*
fresco, ca. 60 × 70 cm
Sala del Trono, Palazzo Patriarcale, Udine

a very late date, posterior to both the Schorr and titianesque portraits.[28] It could be a portrait painted shortly before his death in the 1690s or perhaps even posthumously, in the first decade of the eighteenth century. This work is attributed to the sole hand of Domenico Tintoretto.[29] With the two aforementioned works it makes up a trio of images linked together by "variations on the theme": for example, the Schorr and Grimani portraits are quite similar (note the almost complete overlap of the brushstrokes of the folds of the robe) except for the presence of the ring and embroidered cuffs, which we instead find in the titianesque portrait, distinguished from the other two by the rendering of the dress and the already mentioned position of the right arm.

It is also possible to hypothesize the presence of Giovanni Grimani within a number of painted scenes: this is the case, for example, of the bearded

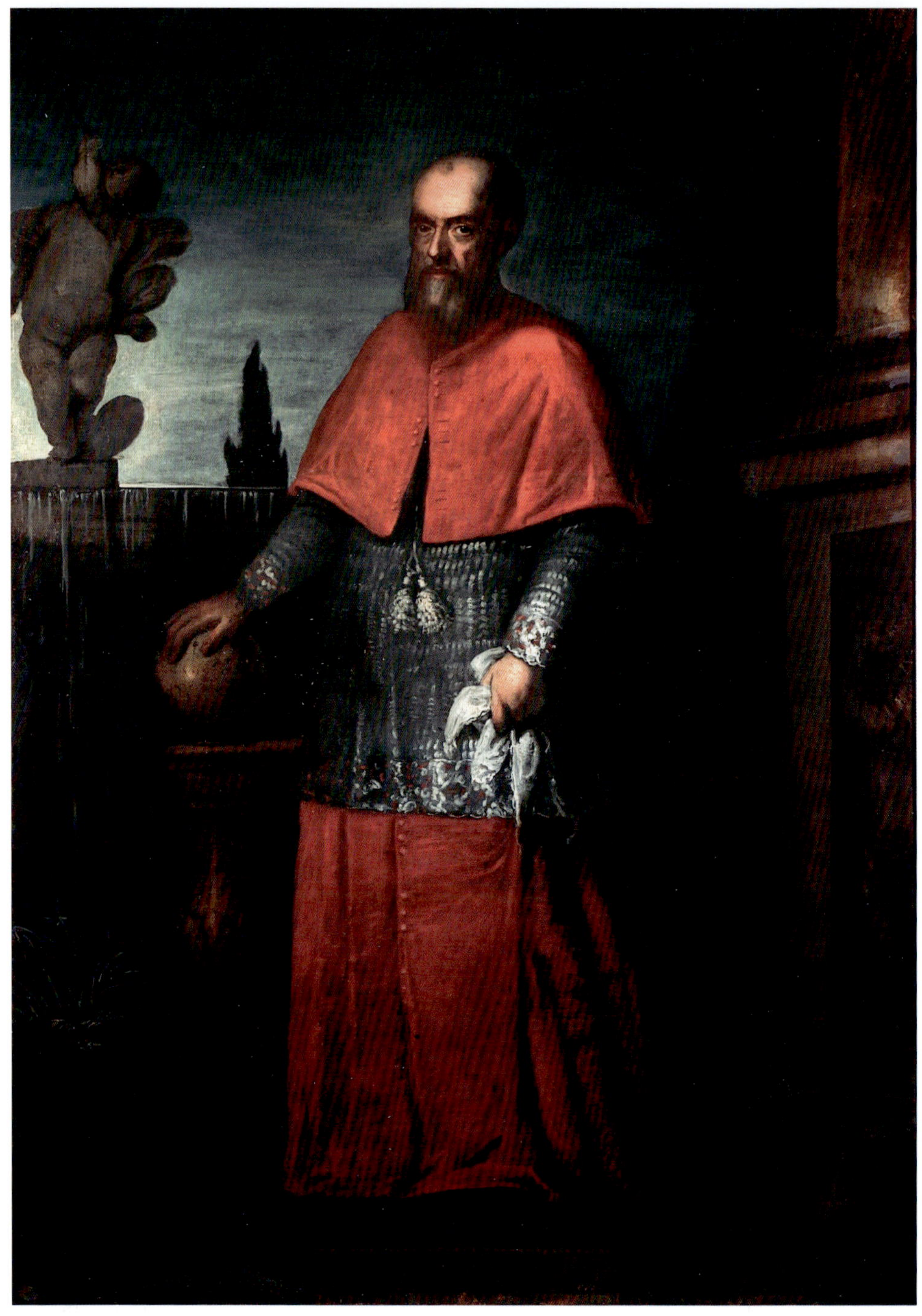

9
Author unknown, *Full-lenght Portrait*
of Giovanni Grimani, seventeenth century
oil on canvas, 240 × 165 cm
unknwon location

old man placed by Federico Zuccari in his *Distributive Justice* (fig. 7) on the stucco and fresco vault of the monumental staircase of Palazzo Grimani, painted around 1565. The character's features are indeed reminiscent of Giovanni—the white beard, the receding hairline—but the features are barely sketched, making the identification unsure. On the other hand, the choice of Giovanni as a model would not be surprising, since the iconographic program of the staircase was certainly decided by the patriarch and has always been considered closely linked to his personal life as prelate and patron (although a recent study[30] suggests a broader iconological reading).

Giovanni might also be present, along with his brothers and perhaps other family members, in Pedro Campaña's *Conversion of Magdalene*, kept in the National Gallery (oil on panel, 29.8 × 58.6 cm) (cf. p. 66), a painting certainly commissioned by the family. If so, he would be the bearded figure found on the left of the scene, his gaze turned on the viewer. The analysis of this painting is the subject of Francesco Trentini's contribution in this catalog, and so we refer to his article for further information.

Giovanni Grimani is present, this time without any uncertainty since he is explicitly mentioned in the accompanying inscription, in the series of fresco portraits of patriarchs in the throne room of the Patriarchal Palace in Udine (fig. 8).[31] The effigy follows, in chronological succession, those of his uncle Domenico and his brothers Marino and Marco and shows us Giovanni wearing the *mozzetta* and his familiar features, although this time with a rather sullen expression. This image could be an important term of comparison to ascertain the real features of the prelate, keeping in mind, however, that the portraits of Giovanni's uncle and brothers in the series are rather distant from those of other paintings where they surely are present and it is therefore possible that Giovanni was also represented in a manner not entirely "conforming to the original."

Finally, there is one last portrait, at least in the lineup of those known to us, which shows Giovanni Grimani full-length (fig. 9), a format that became common in the seventeenth century. It is one of three paintings by an anonymous author from the Veneto area (but there must have been ten originally) identified by Annalisa Bristot[32] in a private collection (oil on canvas, 240 × 165 cm), which were originally positioned within the stucco frames of the portego of Palazzo Grimani (fig. 10) and depict Giovanni Grimani, along with Pietro (son of Antonio and brother of Domenico) and Marco. This is how Bristot describes the latter:

With a fixed, melancholy gaze, his cheeks hollowed, resting his right [hand] on a balustrade and holding a white handkerchief in his left, the figure in our painting stands out alongside a column on a high carved plinth, against a low wall, on which rests a statue of a putto playing a trumpet, and from which emerges the top of a cypress tree in the twilight sky.[33]

The cassock shows details ("the seventeenth century type stocking and the size of the laces"[34]) that help confirm the dating proposed by Bristot on the basis of stylistic analysis, namely the first decades of the seventeenth century. The painting bears at the bottom the inscription "GIOVANNI GRIMANI PATRIARCH OF AQUILEIA – 1581 – PROMOTED CARDINAL. DIED – 1593 – BEFORE TAKING THE HAT," justifying, here, the use of the cardinal's habit, identical to that of his brother Mark.

Commissioning and collecting the portraits of Giovanni Grimani
One might wonder, at this point, where all these portraits were displayed in the sixteenth and subsequent centuries and who exactly commissioned them, whether Giovanni himself or another member of the family. The painting described by Bristot that we just mentioned, along with the hypothetical portrait in the decorations of the monumental staircase, is the only specimen whose commissioning for the palace is certain. The painting was present there also in 1968, when it appears in a photograph taken for the auction of the property of antiquarian Guido Minerbi, who had for several decades used the building as headquarters for his art dealing business.[35] Mention is made of this work and others in a number of archival and printed documents that may be useful to us in attempting to reconstruct the collecting history of the entire group of portraits already discussed.

The 1784 inventory regarding the *fideicommissum* by Giovanni and Antonio Grimani, preserved at the State Archives of Venice,[36] in fact lists

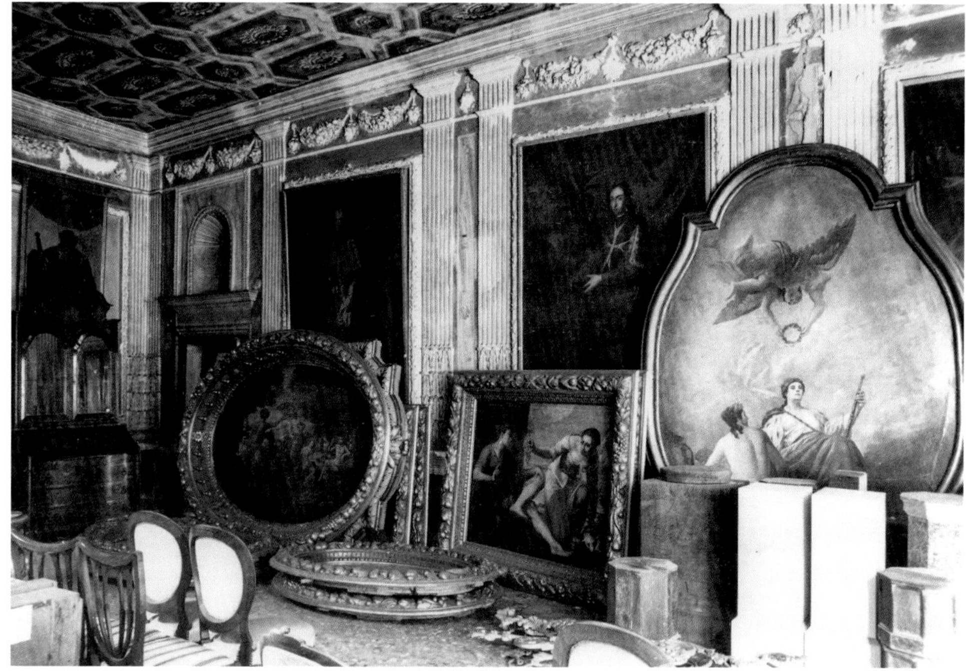

10
The Portego of Palazzo Grimani in the 1960s,
with the works of the antiquarian Minerbi
Photo Archive of Soprintendenza ABAP
per il Comune di Venezia e Laguna

"Standing portraits of the signor Cardinals and Prelates of the house with *Soasa d'Intaglio* now with golden frieze now entirely painted n. 10 ten," which are certainly those identified by Bristot. It must be noted, however, that there is no mention of these in the 1865 inventory drawn up upon Michele Grimani's death, although it is very likely that the portraits were still in the house in 1882 when the heirs of the now-extinguished branch attempted the sale of the group to the Academy of Fine Arts.[37]

For the other works examined, however, we do not possess precise information and no useful sources can be found before the eighteenth century ones. However, we can assume that at least one portrait of Giovanni Grimani was certainly present in the palace as early as the seventeenth century. In the eighteenth century, paintings showing the most important members of the household were placed in the *Camerino of Apollo* and the *Camerino of Callisto*, as well as used as overdoors. They are cited both in the aforementioned 1784 inventory,[38] and in printed sources that variously report information about the collection of paintings, especially guides to the palace and the city of Venice. Among these it is worth mentioning the late eighteenth century booklet *Pitture e sculture nel Palazzo di Casa Grimani*, published by Antonio Graziosi, perhaps at the request of the family itself, which, in the description of the *Camerino di Apollo*, writes, "the paintings representing the Portraits of some Individuals of the family are by *Titian, Bassano, Tintoretto*, and *Paolo* Veronese"[39] and in that of the *Stanza di Callisto*, "Portraits in the natural state of some Individuals of the family, by *Titian* and other talented painters."

Graziosi is echoed by Giannantonio Moschini in the *Guida per la città di Venezia all'amico delle belle arti*, first published in 1815, who informs us of the presence on " the walls of this room [the *Camerino di Apollo*] . . . of portraits of some individuals of this family, painted, according to the mentioned booklet, by Titian, Bassano da Tintoretto and Paolo Veronese,"[40] while in the adjoining small room he observes "the portraits in the natural state of the most illustrious subjects of this family, done by expert brushes."[41] In his later *Courte description des choses plus remarquables du Palais Grimani à sainte Maria Formosa*, dated 1819, Moschini repeats the same descriptions, specifying with regard to the paintings exhibited in the *Camerino di Callisto* that they are "plusieurs portraits de grandeur naturelle" that "sont l'ouvrage de fameus pinceaux de differents temps. Le *Titien* en a fait quelquns des premiers."[42]

The story of the sale of the portrait now in the Schorr collection provides us with further evidence of the presence of portraits in Palazzo Grimani. In notes dating from 1831, George Vivian mentions "Two Tintoretti. Superb pictures of the family (Cardinals) should I wish to have them."[43] The date of 1828, when the purchase was finalized, is the terminus *ante quem of* the painting's presence in the house. One would assume that it had been there from the beginning, but this cannot in fact be taken for granted, since we know that some works of art arrived at the Santa Maria Formosa mansion following the extinction of the Grimani-Calergi branch, including "Portraits of the majors of the family overdoors no. 4," also listed in the 1784 document, which also reports the inventory of the *fideicommissum* of Vettor Grimani Calergi (1738).

As for the other paintings considered, the information does not allow for solid assumptions. Certainly, we cannot rule out that the portrait now in the Museo Grimani was also originally kept in Palazzo Grimani. We do know that its fate was similar to the Schorr one, given that the tags on the back refer to the late nineteenth century English art market (the firm James Bourlet & Sons) and therefore to a possible purchase by English collectors, who between the mid-nineteenth and the first decades of the twentieth century were indeed the main buyers of the discontinued collections of the Venetian patriciate. Certainly, the artist who painted it must have had the opportunity to see and study the portrait later purchased by George Vivian, given their close resemblance: this could confirm the attribution to Domenico Tintoretto of the later work and thus the execution of the two examples within the same workshop, with the physiognomic deviation motivated by the painter's need to age the prelate's face noticeably, taking as a model the late sixteenth century effigies, also probably present in the house.

Focusing finally on the problem of commissioning, and especially of the small-format portraits and *state* portraits, we may notice that almost all of those considered are attributed to the workshops of Titian and Tintoretto, that is, to artists working in Venice. The preference for local painters is also confirmed by the sources already discussed, where this aspect is greatly emphasized.

This choice might seem inconsistent with the "Roman" taste of the family and especially with the direction taken in the 1630s with regard to commissioning the decorations of the palace, entrusted, as already mentioned, to non-Venetian artists. However, the preference for local workshops can be convincingly explained both on a practical level and in terms of taste. Portraits had to respond to other needs, beyond the pleasure of having images of family members in the main residence. Indeed, "portraits had a public value and were rarely intended for the residence of the patrons. In most cases they were sent as gifts to friends or important political figures, not only in Italy but also beyond the Alps."[44] They could be sent to families related by kinship, on the occasion of important events for the subject or for the entire household (such as the appointment to the patriarchate) and were sometimes made in series with small variations on a single

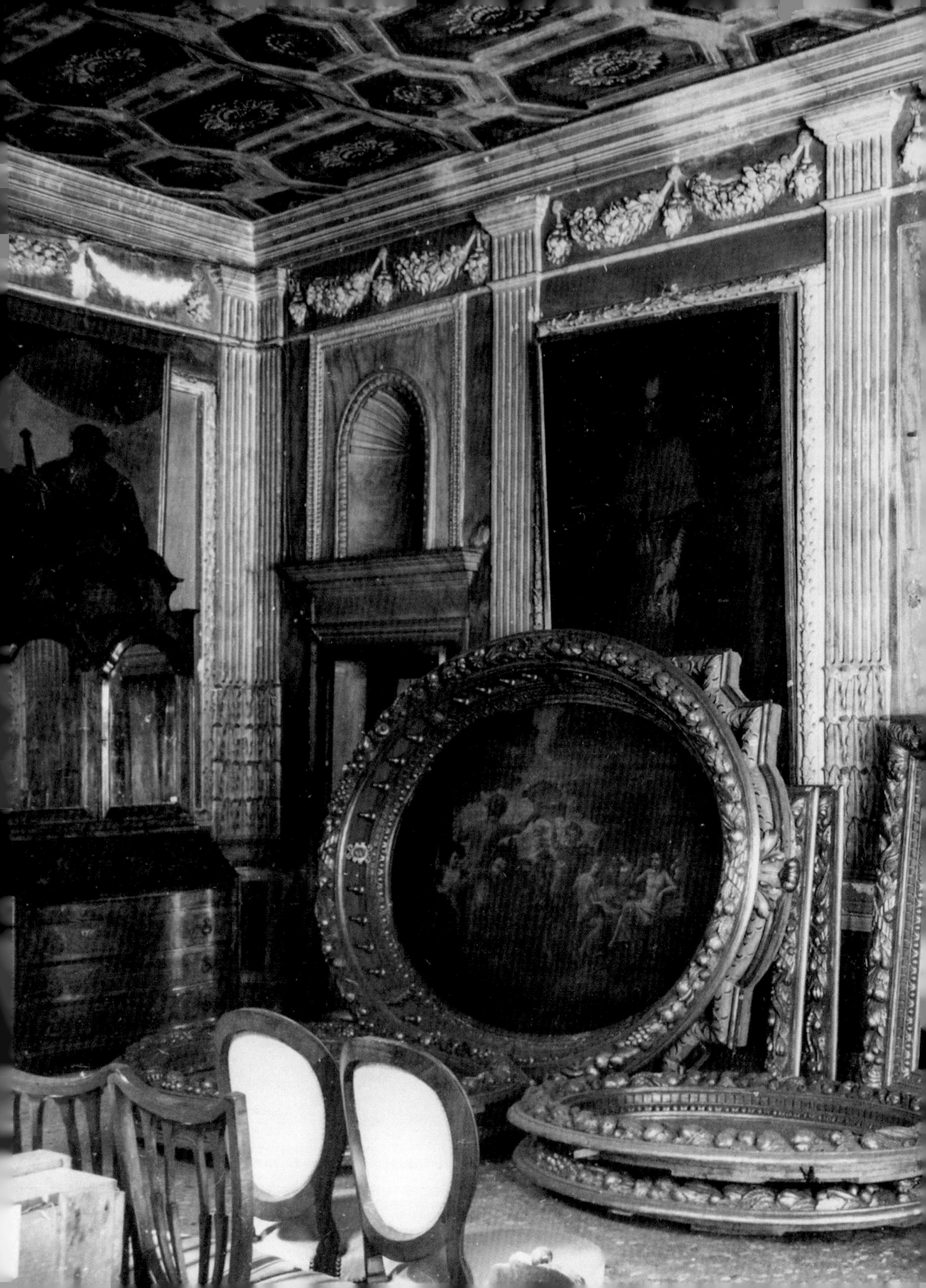

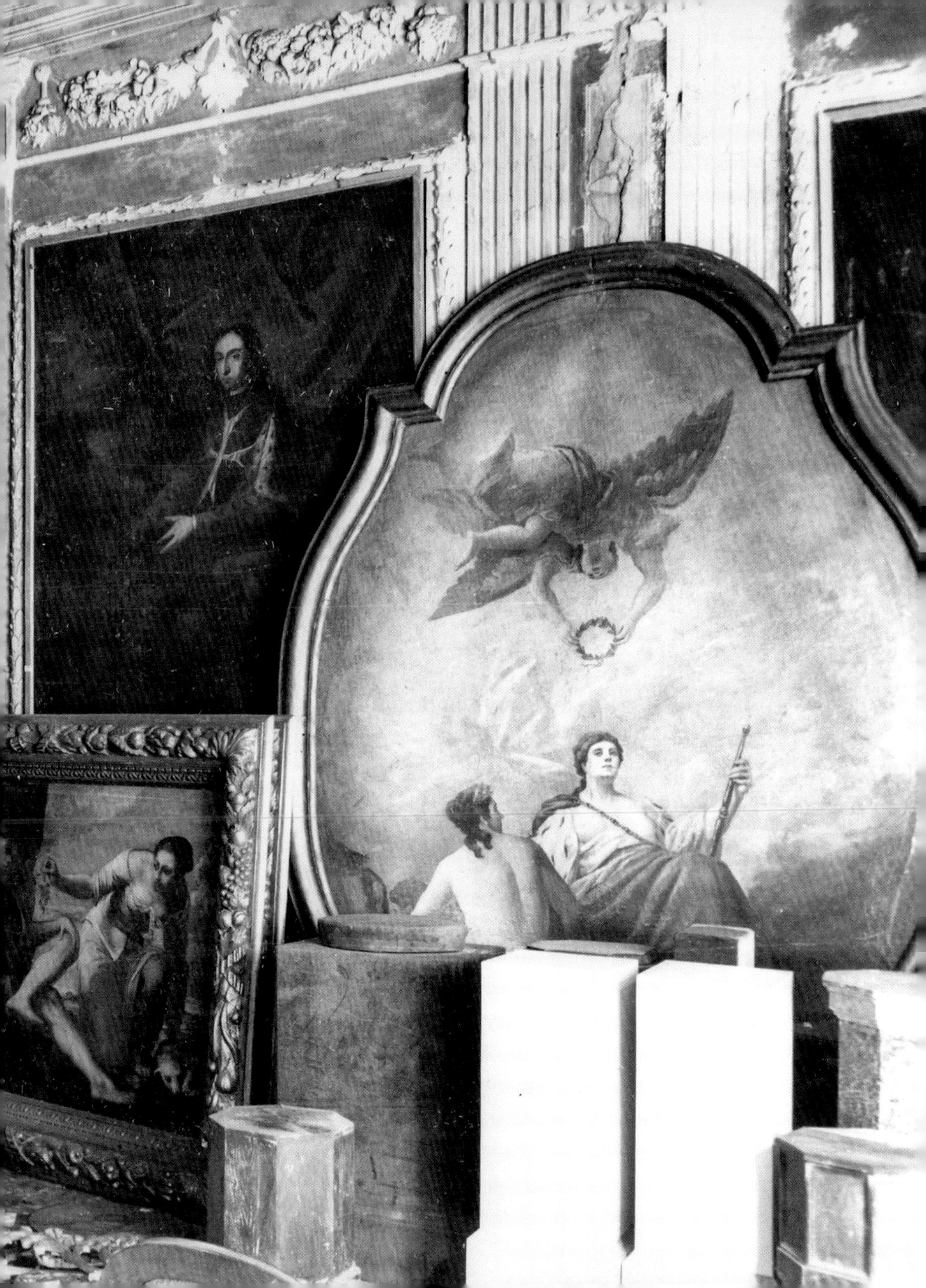

physiognomic model. For all these reasons, proximity was most likely an important factor in choosing the workshops.

By commissioning his portraits from Venetian artists, moreover, Giovanni showed himself attentive to trends in painting production in sixteenth century Italy, since by mid-century the leading position of the Serenissima's masters in portrait-painting was well established.

An exchange of looks with Giovanni Grimani between art, politics and religion

The exact identification of Patriarch Giovanni Grimani in the series of portraits exhibited here certainly constitutes an open problem, appropriately highlighted here. On the one hand, one detects a constant presence of precise physiognomic details in a group of no less than fourteen effigies of Giovanni so far identified, which we have virtually reunited with the two portraits in private collection and Schorr, and with the one exhibited in the Museo di Palazzo Grimani. The above details consist in the subject's extensive baldness interspersed just above the forehead by a few hairs in the three portraits attributable to Jacopo Tintoretto, where the patriarch is shown at very advanced age. The same occurs in the pen-drawn portrait in the Morosini Grimani 270 codex (Library of Museo Correr).[45] Here the author may have taken his cue from Tintoretto's portrait, but combining it with other portraits predating Tintoretto from which he must have taken inspiration for the table covered by a carpet or cloth, laden with objects associated with the patriarch, a composition favored by the Grimani and their circle.[46] In the case of portraits in the Correr manuscript, we find classical fragments and the patriarchal cross on the side of a table, whose surface in the space of the page is only suggested by the coincidence with the footprint of the cursive text. Although not detailed, this pen portrait is significant for its reference to the antiquities collected by the patriarch, used as his attributes: it also worth mentioning how the position of the hand on the subject's chest matches the portrait that Lorenzo Lotto painted for another antiquarian, Andrea Odoni (Royal Collection at Buckingham Palace), although in this case with the introduction of references to the subject's private life. Returning to the physiognomy of the Grimani portraits discussed here, we may note how in all of them the face has strong features, with a protruding cheekbone and hollow cheek, only partially covered by the beard. In all the depictions the mouth has somewhat pronounced lips, while the aspect of the nose varies slightly when moving from the Tintoretto representations to those attributable to another author. In general, it is possible perhaps to identify two different trends in these two groups of portraits both of which must have been to the liking of the patron and his family members, unlike the case of other portraits in the history of art where documents offer evidence of disagreements between patrons and artists. In the case of Giovanni Grimani, this second trend in his depiction characterizes the series referable to a different painter, presumably belonging to the Titian circle, to whom also in the past the qualitatively superior speciments of this smaller group of portraits have been attributed: the cautious attribution of the painting to Domínikos Theotocópoulos by Puppi does not, moreover, appear unconvincing in view of the Greek artist's frequentations with Titian and with Tintoretto, and the contacts the painter had with members of the family both in Crete (the one with Marco Grimani, Duke of Candia, in 1563 is documented) and probably in Venice with Giovanni himself. Also documented is Theotocópoulos' relationship with Giulio Clovio who was also close to and in the service of the family, especially Cardinal Marino.[47] The three portraits, including the one in Palazzo Grimani, offer a slightly different image of the patriarch from the Tintoretto painting, while they resemble the posthumous portrait of Giovanni present in the seventeenth century series that appeared within the frames of the portego of the palace.[48] One detail returns in both trends in the Grimani portraits, the slight rotation of the patriarch's left eye, almost a slight squint, wich is significant for the subject's identification. Summarizing, we may identify an interpretive trend associated with Jacopo Tintoretto in the works depicting Giovanni in an earlier period, while his portraits as an old man seem to belong to a different author, associated with the Titian circle.

The sheer number of coeval portraits of Giovanni Grimani is also significant. It is comparable to that of a doge and one may say proportionate to the political relevance of Giovanni and his family evident in their role in the patriarchate of Aquileia and the bishopric of Ceneda, and in the difficult balance struck between service to the Republic and to the Church, which incidentally may have been an indirect cause of Giovanni's failed cardinalate and his trial for heresy.[49] The figurative and architectural expressions, the iconological 'constructions' of Giovanni Marini, took this role into account. It will suffice to mention the citation in this series of portraits of the ecclesiastical coat of arms located over the ground entrance of Palazzo Grimani. The recovery and reflection on the Antique were by no means generic or neutral actions. They were carried out in service of Venice and for the use of friends, to paraphrase the inscription on the portal of the Palace, with its implicit reference also to the above external contrasts. A truly conscious manifestation of one's role and responsibilities. On the other hand, the whole artistic and collecting enterprise of Giovanni and his predecessors testify to how their public sensibility was also the result of an independent intellectual research, of a profound interest in the humanities as well as in religion: in the latter sphere, our patriarch had to face more than one obstacle including probably that of a Rome-based political clique in his failed bid for the cardinalate.[50]

1 Valeria Finocchi is the author of p. 25 to p. 54; Daniele Ferrara is the author for p. 54 to p. 56.
2 Castelnuovo 1973, p. 1063. For a historical and historiographical reconstruction of the portrait genre see, in addition to Castelnuovo, 1973, the more recent Cieri Via 1989; Buccheri 2010; Bravetti 2019.
3 Ms. 270, Morosini-Grimani fund, Library of Museo Correr. On the volume see the recent Ferrari 2021, pp. 133-142.
4 Antonio was a nephew of Vincenzo, called Spago, brother of Girolamo. His father, therefore, was a first cousin of Giovanni Grimani. It was he who continued the branch of Santa Maria Formosa upon the death of the Patriarch, who had no legitimate descendants.
5 Given the presence of the date of Antonio's death, in January 1627 *more veneto*, it is possible that the last stage of drafting should be postponed by a few months.

6 The medals of the Museo Correr (cl. XXXIX, nos. 4018 and 418, cf. Voltolina 1998, I, no. 696, pp. 716-717) feature on the verso the profile of Marcantonio Barbaro and can be attributed to the foundation of Palmanova (circa 1593), just like the medal of the Civic Museums of Udine, which bears the inscription "IOANNES GRIMANUS PATRIARCA AQUILEIENSIS" on the reverse side.
7 For a complete profile of Giovanni Grimani's life see Benzoni, Bortolotti 2002.
8 See Paschini 1956; Hochmann 2004; Furlan 2014; Samperi 2014.
9 See Paschini 1957; Del Col 2008.
10 Cf. Wolters 2020.
11 See Bristot 2000; Bristot 2001; Craievich 2001; De Paoli 2012.
12 See Zugno 2013; Trentini 2019.
13 Cf. Mallamace 2023.
14 On the Grimani Tribune, and more generally, on the collection of antiquities see: Soccal 2002;

Favaretto 2004; De Paoli 2006-2007; Favaretto De Paoli 2011.

15 Cf. Favaretto 1993 and Favaretto, Ravagnan 1997

16 Cf. Ferrara, Bergamo Rossi 2001.

17 In particular Firpo 2005.

18 The painting was reported to Direzione regionale Musei Veneto and Museo di Palazzo Grimani by the Milan Export Office, where it had been presented for the issuance of the Certificate of Free Circulation. Having ascertained that it was impossible to proceed with a compulsory purchase, the Directorate and the Museum proposed its purchase to the Venetian Heritage Foundation, which concluded the purchase through a private negotiation and donated the painting to the Italian State, also financing a small restoration in view of its exhibition in the *Sala a Fogliami*.

19 It should be pointed out that on the Rikjsmuseum website the painting bears the title *Portrait of a Man with a Red Cloak* and there is no reference to Giovanni Grimani, see https://www.rijksmuseum.nl/nl/collectie/SK-A-2964.

20 Rossi 1973.

21 "The state portrait is the public portrait par excellence. They are large canvases in which the signs of authority and power are explicitly expressed through pose, clothing and symbolic attributes of power", Buccheri 2020, p. 359.

22 The scholar had seen it at Paul Bottenweiser in Berlin, Venturi 1927; Firpo 2005, p. 121 and Tagliaferro in this catalog.

23 See Waagen 1854; Vivian-Neal 1939; Colnaghi 1947; Berenson 1957; Rossi 1974; Pallucchini 1983; Wright 2014 and Tagliaferro in this volume.

24 After several changes of ownership, it was sold in London at Christie's on December 12, 1980, and is now in a private collection, Pallucchini 1983. The collecting vicissitudes of the family at the turn of the eighteenth and nineteenth centuries will be the subject of a forthcoming essay by the author.

25 Pallucchini 1969, II, p. 285.

26 Cf. Puppi 2007.

27 Ibid., p. 423.

28 As moreover reported in Christie's 2004 auction catalog on the basis of an evaluation by Paola Rossi, a scholar of the portraits of the Tintoretto workshop.

29 These are the data with which the portrait was presented to the Milan Export Office in 2020.

30 Mallamace 2023

31 The inventory is kept at the Archivio di Stato di Venezia, Fondo Grimani di Santa Maria Formosa, Busta 5, fasc. 10, document dated January 31, 1784.

32 In appendix to Bristot 2001, pp. 85–88.

33 Ibid., p. 87

34 Ibid.

35 The auction was organized to empty the building and allow it to be sold, probably by Minerbi's heirs. The building was purchased in 1969 by the Olivetti Company.

36 I quote from the document: «Quadri quattro di prelati sopraporte con soaza dorata antichi».

37 The story of the attempted sale of the portraits by the Grimani heirs to the Academy of Fine Arts in 1882 was reconstructed again by Bristot 2001, p. 85.

38 I quote, "Two overdoor portraits with black *soaza*... Paintings four of prelates overdoors with ancient golden *soaza*... A panel portrait with black *soaza*."

39 Titian was the author of a portrait of Doge Antonio Grimani, known from sixteenth century imitations. See Ferrara 2008.

40 Moschini 1815, p. 205.

41 Ibid., p. 207

42 Moschini is most likely referring to the already mentioned portrait of Antonio Grimani, attributed to Titian. Cf. Moschini 1819, p. 60. Moschini mentions the portraits again in the 1828 edition of his *Guida*: Moschini 1828, p. 77.

43 Vivian-Neal 1939, p. 36.

44 Buccheri 2010, p. 343.

45 For a recent review of cardinal portraits and their function, with particular regard to those of the Grimani and the said codex, see again Ferrari 2021.

46 The reference is to the portrait of Domenico Grimani preserved in the Royal Collections at Windsor Castle that Giovanni Shearman considered a possible copy from a model by Lorenzo Lotto (Shearman 1983, p. 149, cat. 145), but also to the portrait of Giovanni Zulian, see Ferrara 2007; Ferrari 2021, pp. 126–28; Hochmann 2021. A portrait of Domenico Grimani attributed to Lorenzo Lotto is also part of the Schorr collection and is preserved at Dublin Castle, see Wright 2014, vol. I, pp. 159–160, no. 217.

47 Puppi 2007.

48 Bristot 2001.

49 Pin 1983, pp. 252, 274; Tafuri 1994, pp. 6–7, 12–13, 29–30. See also https://www.treccani.it/enciclopedia/il-pubblico-e-il-privato-architettura-e-committenza-a-venezia_%28Storia-di-Venezia%29/.

50 Trentini 2019.

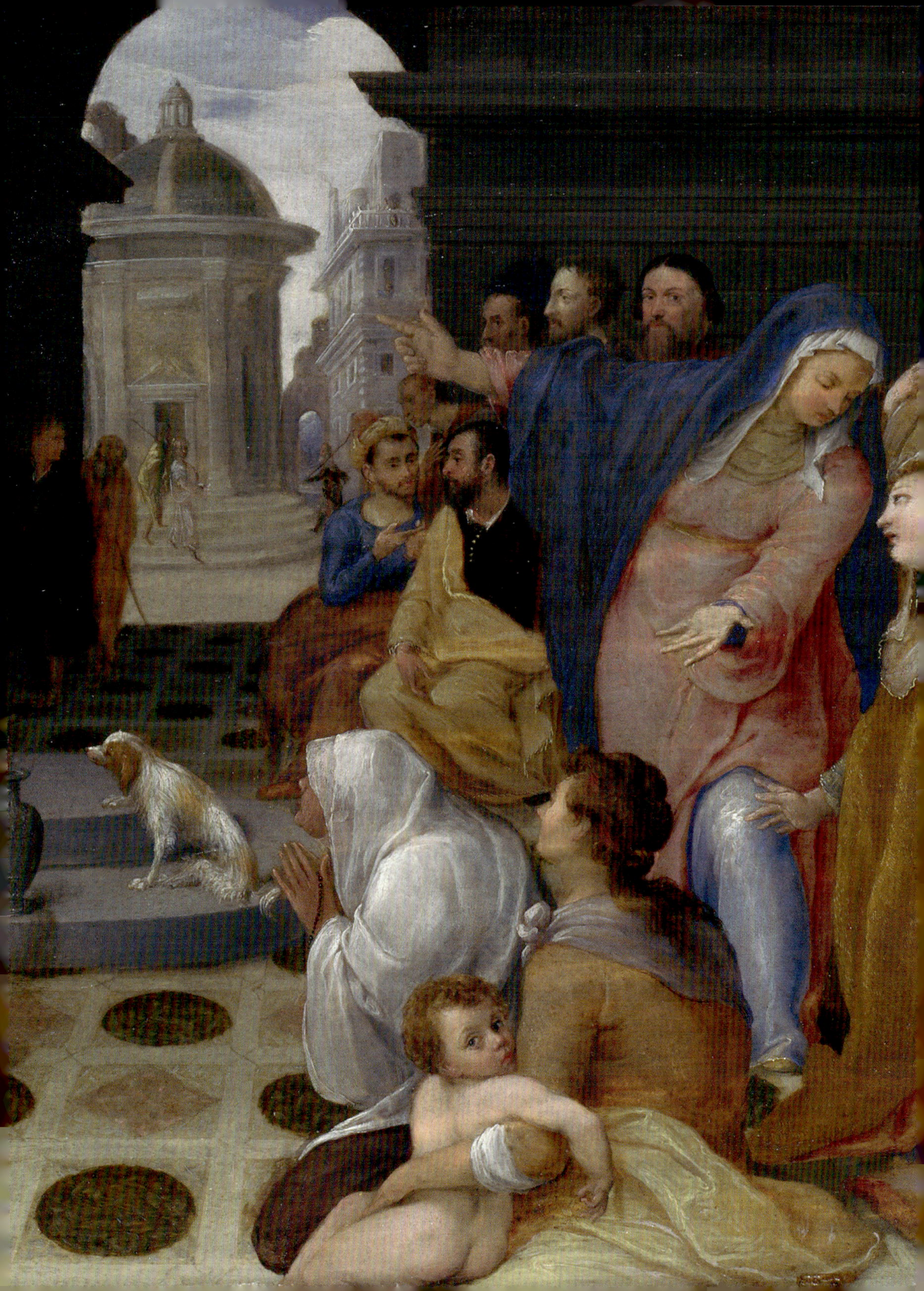

"Truly and effectively cardinal": Giovanni Grimani and his red *mozzetta*

Francesco Trentini

There is a dominant color associated with the life and person of Giovanni Grimani: purple. The color of sublimity and suffering, the color of blood and of power. Following the death of his brother Marino, Giovanni Grimani had become titular patriarch of Aquileia, a position he would retain for the rest of his life, although he availed himself from 1550 to 1585 of two coadjutors: Daniel Barbaro first and Aloisio Giustiniani later. He would certainly have worn the red mozzetta, granted *ab antiquo* by the pontiffs to the Aquileian patriarchs to symbolically affirm their ideal proximity to the status of cardinal. But color alone is not enough. Cardinals were given far more prerogatives and power than a patriarch of Aquileia could boast. In particular: the right of *renuntiatio cum regressu*, i.e., the possibility of renouncing certain offices in favor of people of their own choosing (a formidable tool for maintaining solid political networks) and of course the right to participate in the conclave that appointed the pope.

His uncle Domenico and his brother Marino had both all become cardinals. But for Giovanni things turned out differently. Attracted at least as much as uncle Marino by the religious unrest that had surfaced also in the Catholic world in the wake of the Reformation crisis, Giovanni got naively caught up in the nascent network of Roman control and inquisition, the institutional expression of a religious world recoiling against the Protestant rebellion, a world whose views were to be dramatically reaffirmed a few decades later with the counter-reformation. A first charge of heresy brought against him in 1547 by Bishop Dionigi Zanettini of Milopotamos forced Giovanni to undergo a first "purgatione" in Rome, in 1551–1552. He was absolved and rehabilitated, but the suspicions were never fully allayed and were enough to motivate a rejection by Pope Julius III of Giovanni' bid for cardinalate. Ten years later, in early 1561, the efforts and diplomatic skill of the Venetian ambassador Marcantonio Da Mula managed to secure from Pius IV's a cardinalate "in pectore. The full position seemed now a done thing, but the plan unraveled following a new accusation of heresy, launched on the eve of the promotion of the new cardinals. The matter was serious, and Giovanni was again forced to defend himself in person in the Holy Office in Rome: at this point it was no longer just a matter of promotion, his very personal safety depended on the outcome, which was successful but again prevented him from achieving the position.

Historiography has seen fit to insist on Giovanni's personal aspiration for the cardinalate and his deep frustration at his failure, seeing his patronage of the arts in part as a form of compensation. But was it really a matter of personal ambition, of a delusional obstinacy which led him to mobilizing the Venetian political leadership in his favor? If indeed this was the case his frustration must have certainly been eased by the fact that for the Republic of Venice from an early moment, indeed from the early 1560s—as Tiberio Deciano was to declare, Giovanni Grimani was "truly and effectively cardinal."[1]

Deciano's aside was not an occasional piece of flattery: along with him, also Marco Mantova Benavides and Girolamo Tornielli, the leading juridical experts in Padua of the time, both wrote reports in which they demonstrated and declared that Grimani should be considered to all intents and purposes a cardinal, since he lacked only the last proclamation, which had been postponed but not denied, just as his *de facto* inclusion in the cardinal lists, albeit *in pectore*, had also never been officially rejected.[2] Little relevance was to be given, Marco Cavina explained, to counter arguments that relied on improper analogies between canon law and civil criteria.[3] In substance, the Venetian Republic considered Giovanni Grimani's election to cardinal as valid, with all its consequences, *in primis* the right to enter the conclave for the election of the future pontiff and then all the "alia iura" associated with the cardinalate.[4]

A different view of Giovanni Grimani's attitude emerges however from the rich documentation existing on the case, as soon we discover the considerable pressure exerted by the Venetian Republic not only on the Roman Curia but also on Giovanni himself, who ends up appearing in his institutional and judicial movements almost a pawn in a superior political strategy. If we look carefully we notice that, already in 1548, it was an injunction by the Venetian government and not Giovanni's initiative that sparked the negotiations for the appointment of a successor that resulted in Giovanni's renunciation in favor of the elected of Aquileia, Daniele Barbaro. Also impressive was the diplomatic initiative taken by the Serenissima in support of Giovanni's appointment as cardinal, a case entrusted to the care of the Venetian ambassador Domenico Morosini as early as February 1555 and then to that of his successor Bernardo Navagero in the same year. The energy with which the Republic pursued this goal was evident also to Pope Julius III who noticed how unusual it was for the Serenissima to spend itself at these levels for a personal case: "vedemo una continua volontà della Signoria verso la persona sua, *cosa che, per quel che si potiamo raccordar, non si sol far.*" (we notice a continue interest of the Republic in your person, which, from what we can remember is not usually done).[5] Moreover, it was not Giovanni but the Venetian Senate who in 1561 charged the Serenissima's consul, Tiberio Deciano, with the mission of defending Grimani in the dispute in Rome.[6] One should note in this regard the existence of an official act presented to the Council, signed and consecrated with his own seal by Deciano, in which the jurisconsult argued with legal vigor "that the most illustrious Giovanni Grimani Patriarcha d'Aquileia is truly and effectively a cardinal, and by right must be admitted to the election of the future pontiff."[7]

The Serenissima's insistence can be explained if one considers the very delicate position of the Patriarchate of Aquileia in the geopolitical balances between the Empire and the Republic. The awarding to the current patriarch of the title of cardinal would have given the Serenissima a stability that was crucial in an area so delicate for the maintenance of its territorial and political balance with the Empire, since the *potestas cardinalicia*

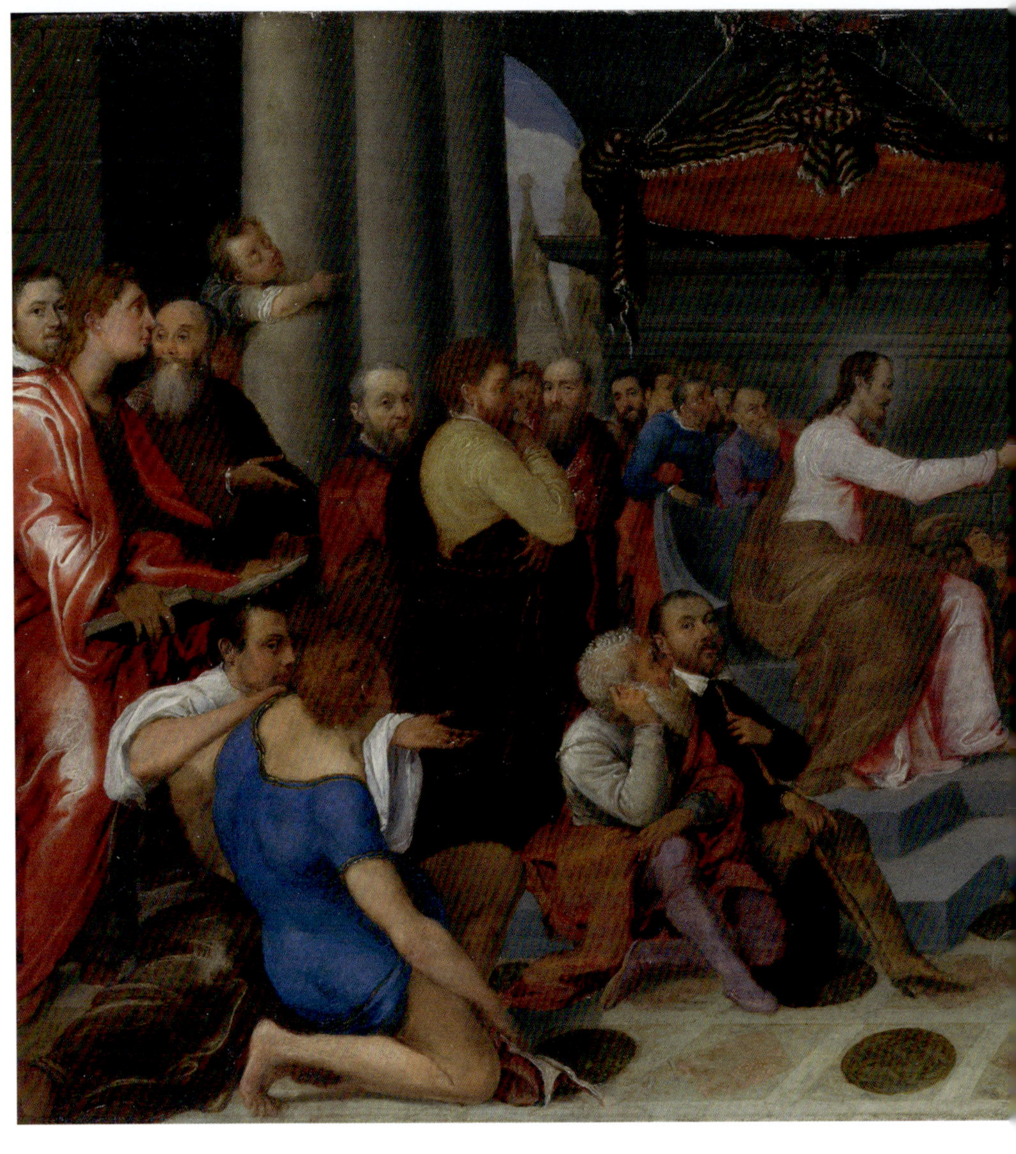

1
Pedro Campaña,
The Conversion of Mary Magdalene,
ca. 1562
oil on panel, 29.8 × 58.4 cm
The National Gallery, London,
Bought, 1888

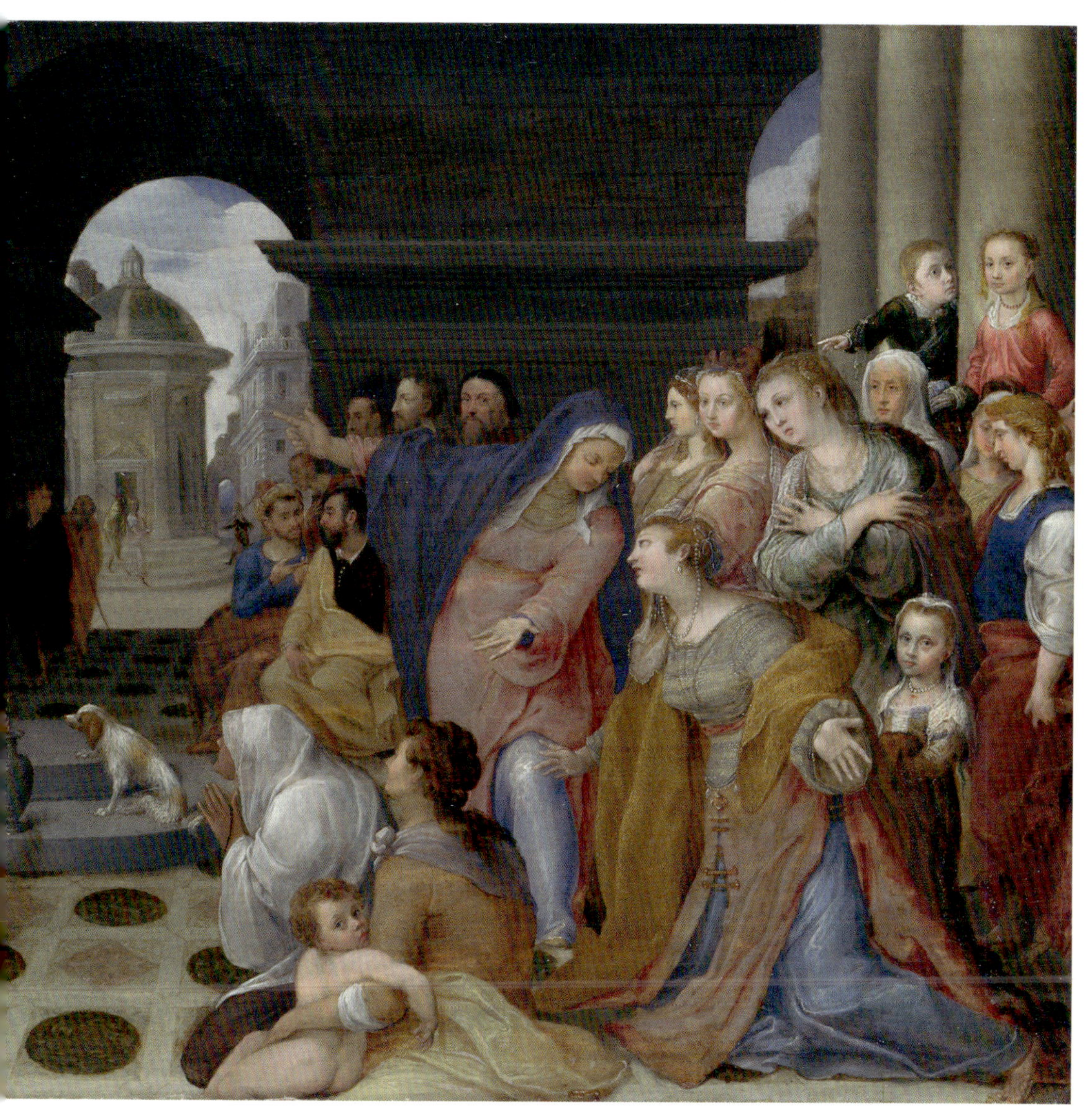

would certainly have helped the Republic when it came to designate the future patriarch, allowing it to maintain its control over Aquileia and the Patria of Friuli through a firm succession of subjects loyal to the Republic. Only as a cardinal could Giovanni have enjoyed the right of renunciation and regression.[8] It was important, therefore, for the Grimani family to insist on Giovanni's status as cardinal through the iconography of the portraits also out of a political obligation to the Venetian state, which had saw fit to permanently ratify what in Rome was intended to be kept perpetually *sub iudice*. Thus the presence in the paintings of the red *mozzettas* to be understood as cardinal hats, not only in public portraits but also in private one, not a surprising fact given that in Venice the private sphere had necessarily to be managed at certain levels with an eye for political implications.

Although no doubt a serious issue that weighed heavily on his life, the matter of the cardinalate, however, did not wholly permeate Giovanni's private sphere. It had been the rancorous Dionigi Zanettini, bishop of Milopotamos and Chiron, who had enriched the accusation of heresy with the insinuation that Giovanni Grimani had aims on the cardinalate,[9] perhaps embroidering on an actual policy imposed on Giovanni by the Venetian leadership. Indeed, from a letter to his brother Vettore dated April 19, 1550, we learn how much the prospective cardinalate was felt by Giovanni as a burden,[10] an attitude that seems confirmed by the emblematic cycle in the *Sala a Fogliami* in Palazzo Grimani, decidedly risqué when it came to theological and "spiritual" issues,[11] in line with the not exactly diplomatic sensibility of a man who, as Carnesecchi recalled, "parlava voluntieri et liberamente delle cose che sono in controversia della religione" (spoke willingly and freely of things that are controversial in religion)[12]. A valuable panel painting in the National Gallery in London (fig. 1) attributed to the Spaniard naturalized Flemish painter Pedro Campaña showing the conversion of Mary Magdalene may help understand this "spiritual" side of Giovanni. The small work can be confidently referred to the Grimani circle given the presence of the unmistakable portrait of Giovanni's brother, Procurator Vettor Grimani (fig. 2), peeping out on the right just above Martha's outstretched arm.[13] In the jumble of endless details, one cannot help noting the small intense face of a man of perhaps sixty positioned

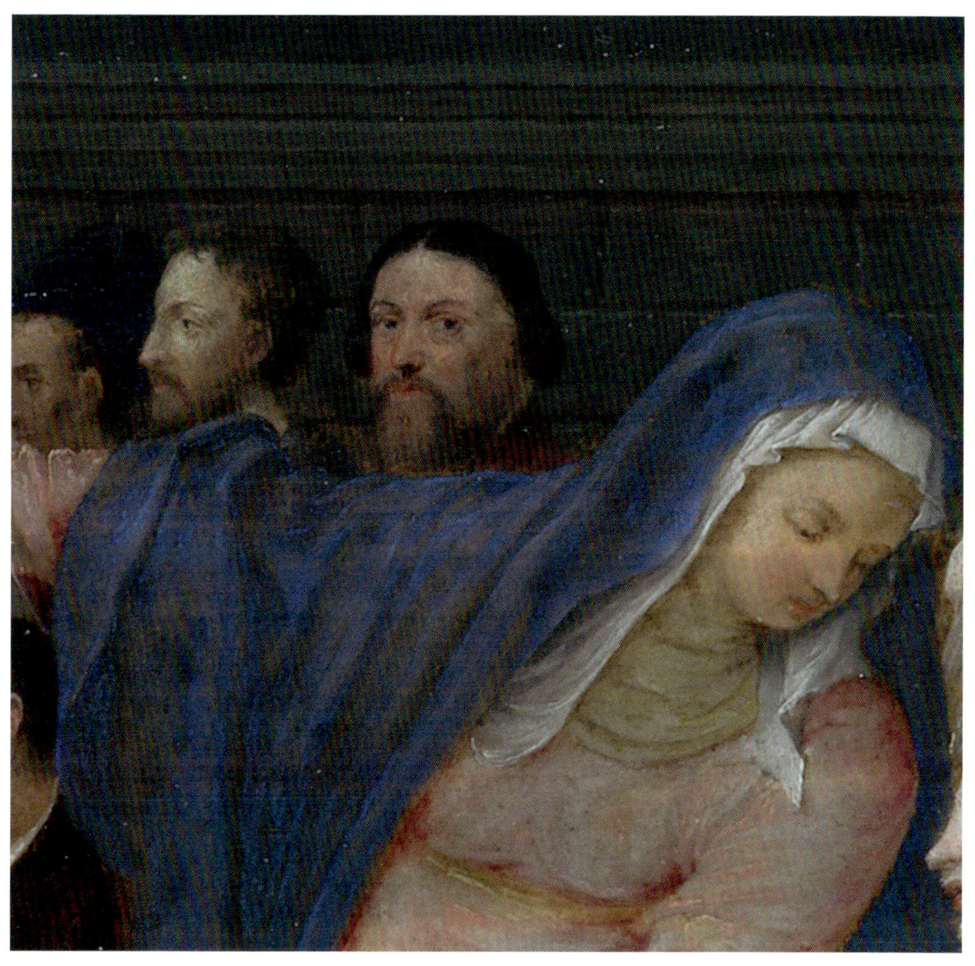

2
Pedro Campaña,
The Conversion of Mary Magdalene,
detail, ca. 1562
The National Gallery, London

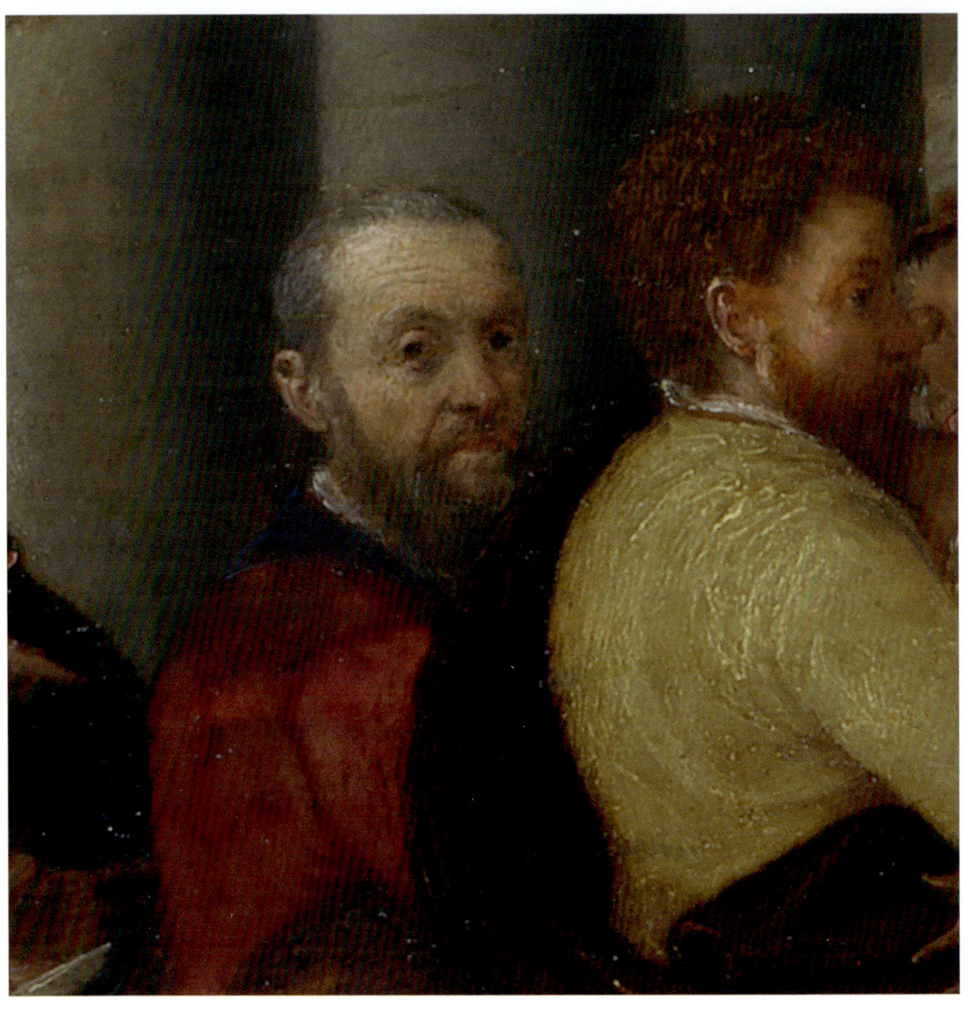

3
Pedro Campaña,
The Conversion of Mary Magdalene,
detail, ca. 1562
National Gallery, London

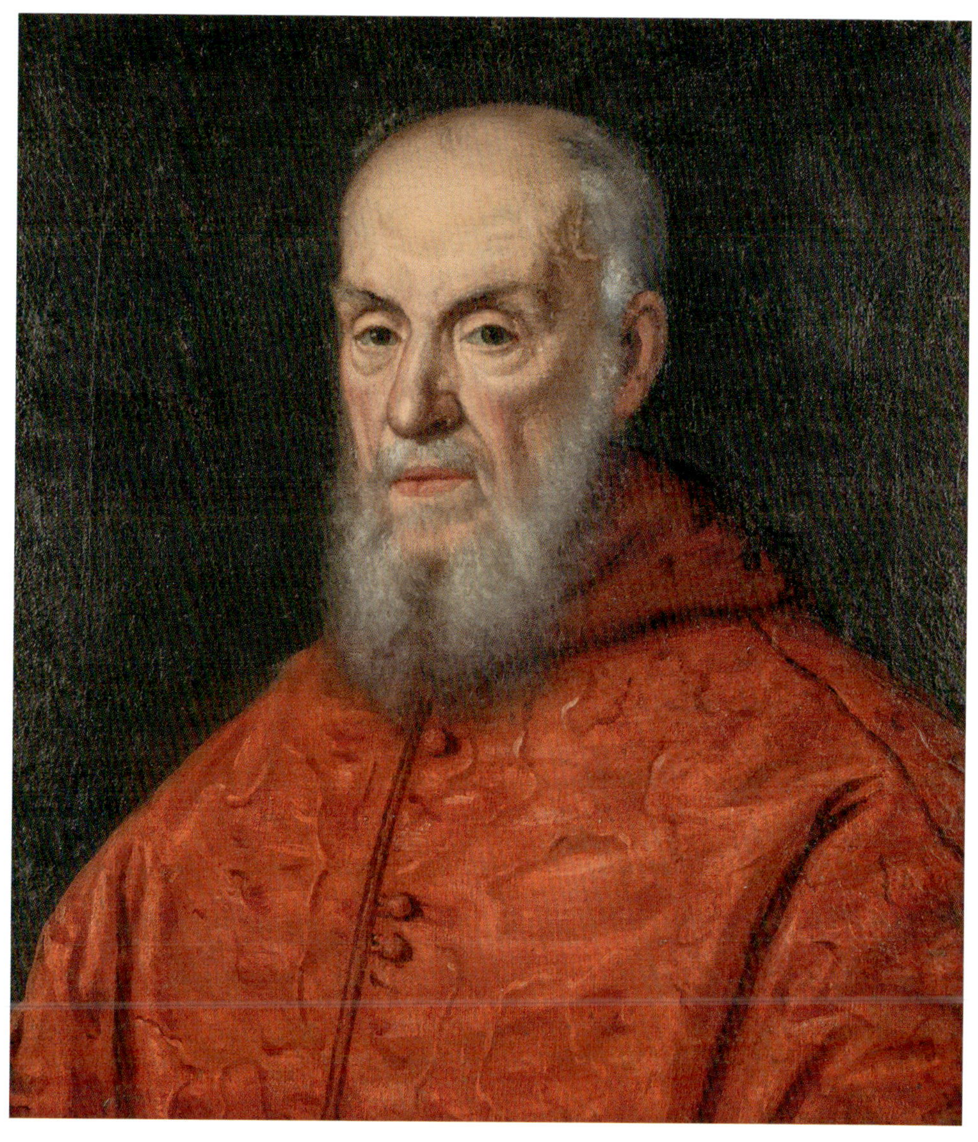

4
Jacopo and Domenico Tintoretto (attr.),
*Portrait of Giovanni Grimani, Patriarch
of Aquileia*, ca. 1590–1593
Oil on canvas, 57.4 × 50 cm
Museum Soumaya, Fundación Carlos
Slim Collection, Mexico City

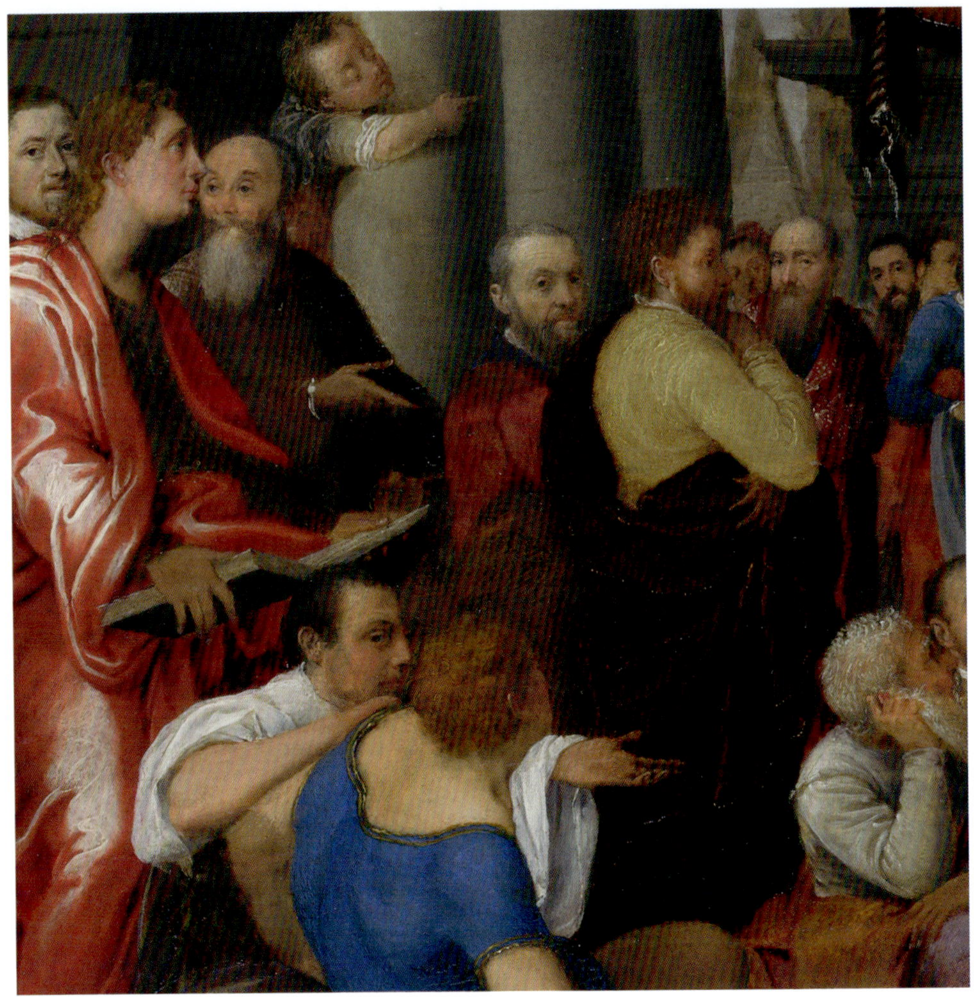

5
Pedro Campaña,
The Conversion of Mary Magdalene,
detail, ca. 1562
The National Gallery, London

on the left under a section of colonnade, intent on scrutinizing the viewer with a firm gaze (fig. 3). The impression is of being in front of the same man who, having aged, had posed in cardinal's robes for the portrait in the Museum Soumaya in Mexico City (fig. 4): the same large eyelid, the slightly pronounced eyeballs framed by large bags, the same curved, low cheekbone, the same falling cheek—a little more in the Sotheby portrait, a little less in Campaña—and finally that fleshy mouth with the slightly protruding lower lip. Could this, then, have been the face of Giovanni Grimani around 1560? Mere physiognomic evidence, as it is known, can be extremely misleading. What is most likely, however, is that the name of the mysterious gentleman must have indeed been named Giovanni, based on the following semiotic clue: in the painting, a balding elderly man with a long beard and cerulean eyes is turning towards the figure of the evangelist John (inserted in the scene with Mary Magdalene by virtue of an apocryphal tradition taken up even by Domenico Cavalca who claimed them to be betrothed or even husband and wife (here, however, the evangelist is already wearing the red mantle of divine Charity and carrying a gospel in his hands). The old man, we were saying, is looking at the evangelist John (in Italian "Giovanni") and meanwhile is pointing his index finger at our middle-aged man, thus establishing a connection between the two men (fig. 5), a connection that is most likely the common name.[14]

We should note finally that, in this painting totally geared towards the "spiritual" themes dear to Giovanni Grimani—the large way of mercy, the benefit of Christ, predestination, the warm tears of the Magdalene that wash the soul and justify through faith—we find no reference whatsoever to the institutional issue of his cardinalate, confirming, perhaps, the lack of interest in the position that Giovanni had expressed to his brother Vettore in the letter written ten years earlier.

Extraordinarily cardinal-like, albeit very direct and intimate, is instead the portrait in the Museum Soumaya, perhaps traceable back to the circle of Bassano. Given its half-length format and the intensity of the gaze directed at the viewer shows that it is pursuing a decisive attenuation of the institutional features characteristic of official ecclesiastical portraiture. Although he must have been close to eighty, Giovanni's face still shows a significant muscular tone, as, moreover, has already been noted by historiography.[15] One may wonder what circumstance may have motivated Giovanni to commission the work, which chronologically must have come in the aftermath of the settlement of a serious crisis between the prelate and the Venetian state occasioned by a mishandling of the dispute over the succession of the fief of Taiedo.[16] While it is true that the donation of the Statuary to the Republic may be viewed as an attempt to settle the conflict, it is possible that Giovanni had thought of accompanying the donation with the commission of a portrait having a memorial function. What about the cardinal's purple in the painting. Well, since Venice had ratified his cardinalate, it could not have been otherwise. It was the Republic that wanted the *de facto* cardinalate, Giovanni knew it as did all the players in the Venetian political arena and therefore the reference was coherently present in the painting. Indeed, it is following the same political logic that, in the funeral oration for Giovanni Grimani addressed to the Venetian Senate, the philosopher Fabio Paolini from Udine summarized Giovanni's *cursus honorum* as following: "Abbot of Sesto, then appointed bishop of Ceneda, then Patriarch of Aquileia, finally also Cardinal."[17]

1 Ms. Malvezzi 152, cc. 239v–242v (239v), Biblioteca del Museo Correr, Venice.

2 Deciani 1602, Resp. VIII, cc. 65r–78v. Cf. Cavina, 2004, pp. 264–55.

3 Cavina 2004, p. 251.

4 So reads a response by Girolamo Tornielli published in Deciani 1602, c. 77v, col. b.

5 ASVe, Consiglio dei Dieci (Capi), b. 24, no. 19, c. [1]r (italics are mine).

6 Cavina 2004, p. 248.

7 Ms. Malvezzi 152, c. 239v-242v, Biblioteca del Museo Correr, Venice.

8 Laven 1966–67, pp. 184–205 (187).

9 Benzoni, Bortolotti 2002, pp. 613–21.

10 The document is commented in Trentini 2019, pp. 267–90 (269–72).

11 Trentini 2019, pp. 281–89.

12 Firpo, Marcatto 1988, p. 188.

13 Almost palpable is the similarity with the portrait still in the family chapel at Santa Maria Formosa, on which is inscribed "VIETORE/ GRIMAN/ PROCURAT/ S.TO MARCE" in a rather improbable Latin, and with the counterpart in the Gallerie dell'Accademia (inv. no. 1968) bearing the inscription "VICTOR GRIMANO M.D.XXII."

14 According to similar logic of association "a rebus," one must then ask whether the thick-bearded man showed just beyond Giovanni Grimani, immediately to the left of the pensive young man in a yellow suit, having been placed immediately below a gash in the architectures open to two pyramids, one of which is decorated with hieroglyphics, might not be a *posthumous* portrait of Giovanni Grimani's brother, Marco Grimani, famous for his archaeological interests and for having entered the pyramid of Cheops. See Davis 2011, n.p.

15 Cf. Firpo 2005, pp. 825–71 (868–69) and Pancheri 2009, pp. 311–13.

16 Benzoni, Bortolotti 2002, pp. 613–21.

17 Paolini da Udine 1593, c. [5]r: "... ut primum factus Sexti abbas, mox Cenetensis episcopus creatus, tum Aquileiensis patriarcha, postremo etiam cardinalis, cuius quidem dignitatis gradum ita est assecutus, ut summi ac optimi Pontificis dignus sit habitus et designatus." The passage goes on to praise the caution of Grimani who, despite having been granted the dignity of cardinal, feared "malevolent invitations" and therefore had, as it were, suspended the office until his innocence and the calumnies of others had been shown. See Firpo 2005, pp. 866–67 and Pancheri 2009, pp. 311–13.

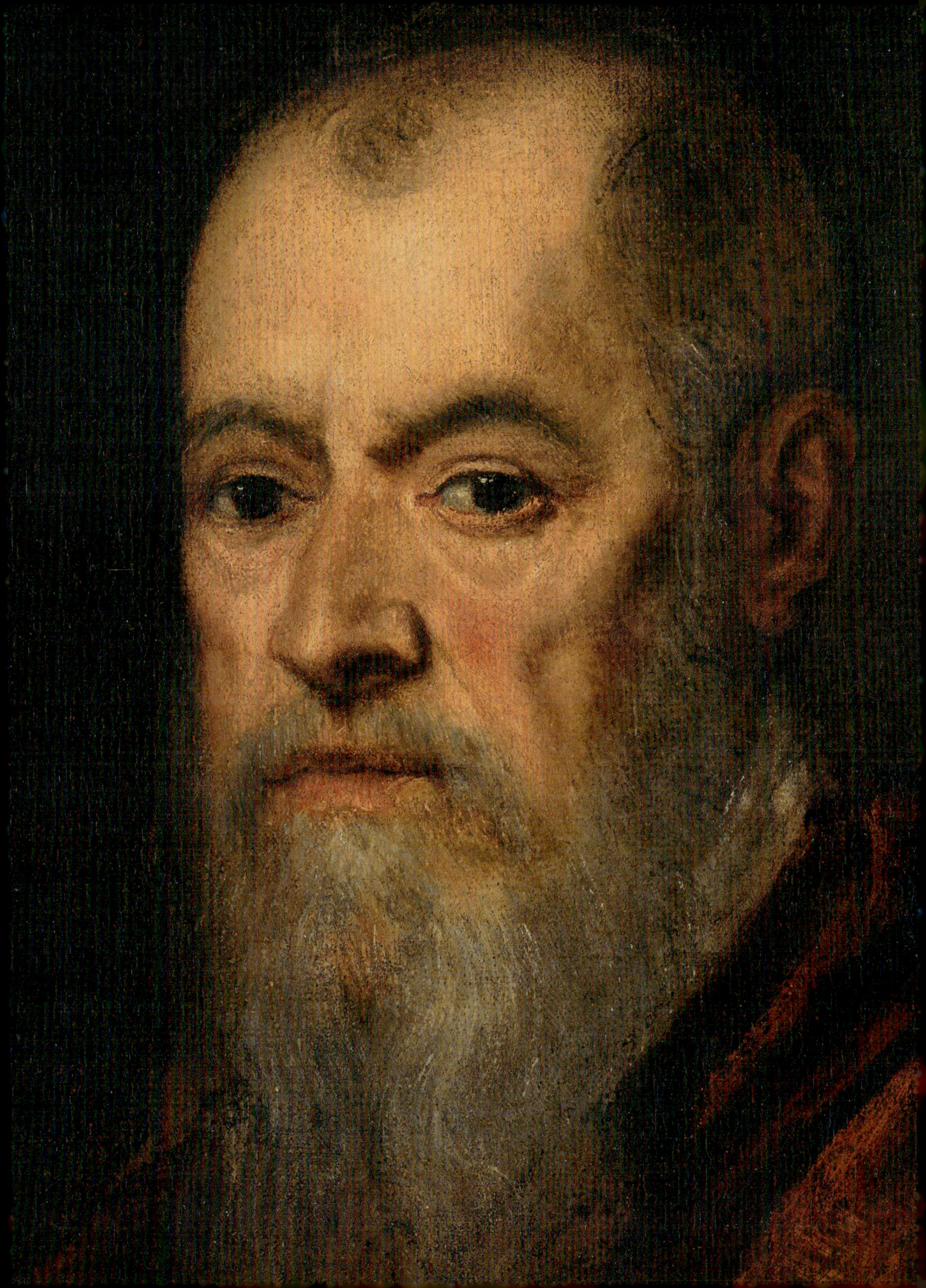

Jacopo Tintoretto's Portrait study of Patriarch Giovanni Grimani

Giorgio Tagliaferro

The small panel painting discussed in this essay and publicly displayed for the first time in the present exhibition (oil on panel, 57,5 × 40,5 cm) (fig. 1) portrays a man who looks approximately between his 50s and 60s. He is shown at nearly three-quarter length and seated in an armchair, with his left arm resting on the armrest and the right one stretched along the body. The lower margin of the panel cuts the figure just below the waist and partly crops the fingers. The sitter is positioned diagonally at 45 degrees from the surface plane, with the head slightly rotated so that he makes eye contact with the viewer. He wears a buttoned up, red hooded cape (*mozzetta*) over a white tunic (*rocchetto*) similar to a surplice. This is the typical dress of sixteenth century cardinals; the figure, though, lacks the distinctive red cap or biretta and ring that should complement his vestments. The figure stands out against a neutral, dark brown background, with a curtain pulled back to the right behind the sitter's back. The man's self-assured gaze and imposing physical and mental presence convey the sense of a strong-minded personality. This, along with the prestige of the ecclesiastical dignity, urges questions about the identity of the sitter and the context in which the painting was produced. In this regard, whereas its original provenance remains unknown to date, its evident connection with another portrait sheds some light on the person portrayed, as argued in this essay. The earliest known mention of the painting dates from

1927, when it was in the hands of the Berlin-based antiquarian Bottenwieser. Adolfo Venturi viewed the picture at that time and published it as a work by Jacopo Tintoretto, followed by Georg Biermann.[1] Only two years later it was referred to by Hans Gronau as in a private American collection.[2] At an unknown date, it became a property of Luigi Pellino (d. 1997) in Rome, and was eventually inherited by his daughter Tullia. Since these early mentions in the late 1920s, the painting has not appeared in the literature. It has never been displayed publicly before the present exhibition, and is discussed here for the first time.

Analysis of the painting, identity of the sitter, authorship

The small portrait is executed with great care in the areas of the face and of the red *mozzetta*. The solid volume of the head is blocked out through a confident use of the line, which silhouettes the right side of the face (to our left) against the background, gently following the bulging contours of the forehead, eyebrow, and cheekbone. The strong line of the eyebrows arch and firm design of the nose give stability to the composition of the facial features. The pool of light on the nose tip, the deep recession of the nostrils and the shadow cast by the nose on the area above the lips give relief to the figure. The sagging of the cheeks, contrasted by the protrusion of the left cheekbone, creates a chiaroscuro effect that enhances the volume. These details are rendered with precision and vividness; so is the thin grey hair of the beard (with white highlights) that frames the tightly closed lips. The gaze is very intense, each eyeball vibrantly lit and slightly misaligned to capture the vigour and concentration of the sitter staring before the artist. Considered the immediacy of the sitter's expression, there is little doubt that this portrait was painted from life. Likewise, the *mozzetta* is rendered with highly evocative textural effects. The artist has alternated broader structural strokes that delineate the folds with subtler, abbreviated touches laden with highlights that reproduce the surface effects of the watered fabric. The high level of accuracy signals that the artist endeavoured to present the patron with a realistic and dramatic effigy. By contrast, the lower part of the picture shows less

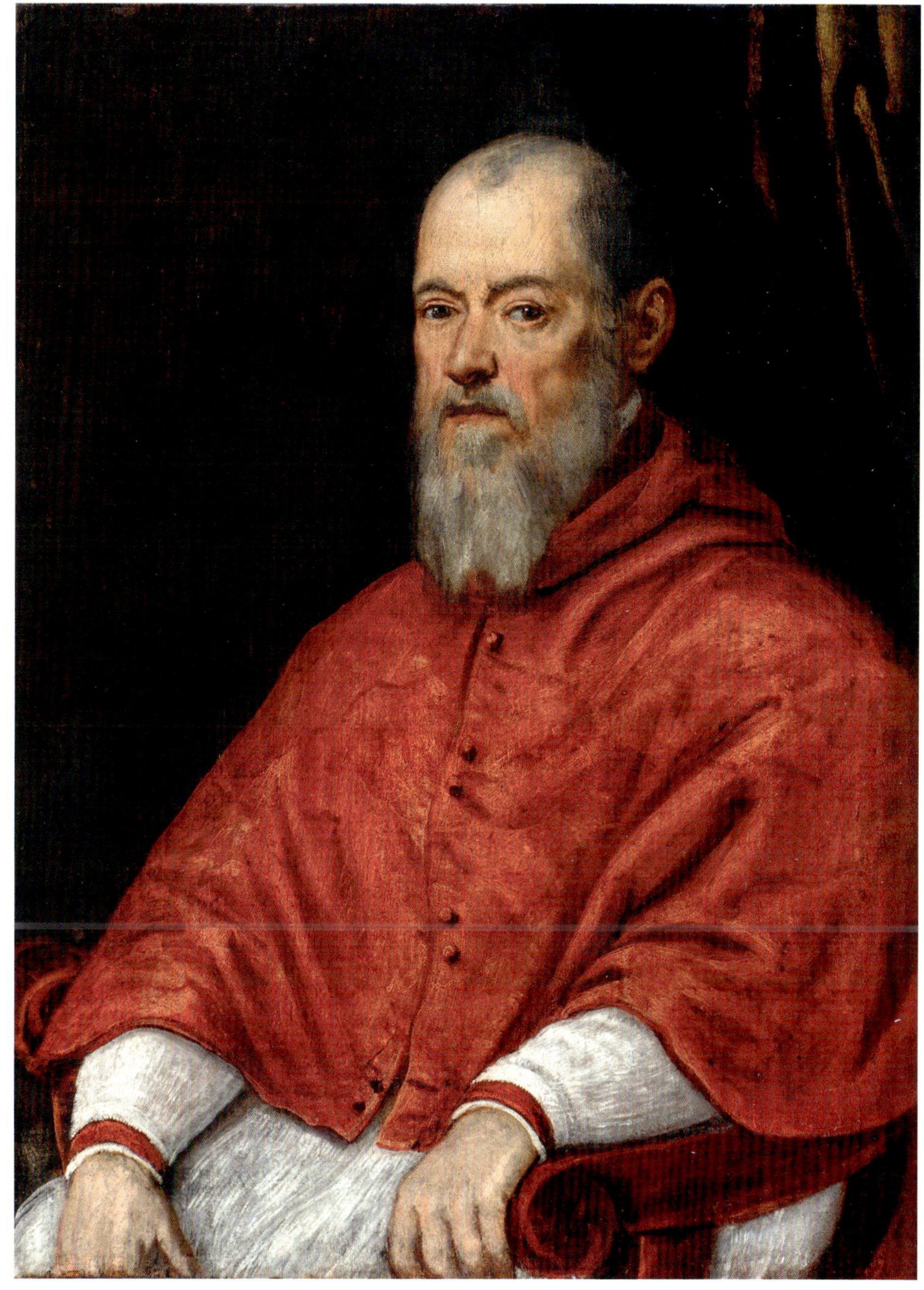

1
Jacopo Tintoretto, *Portrait of Giovanni Grimani*,
second half of the sixteenth century
oil on panel, 57.5 × 40.5 cm
Private collection, sketch of Schorr's painting

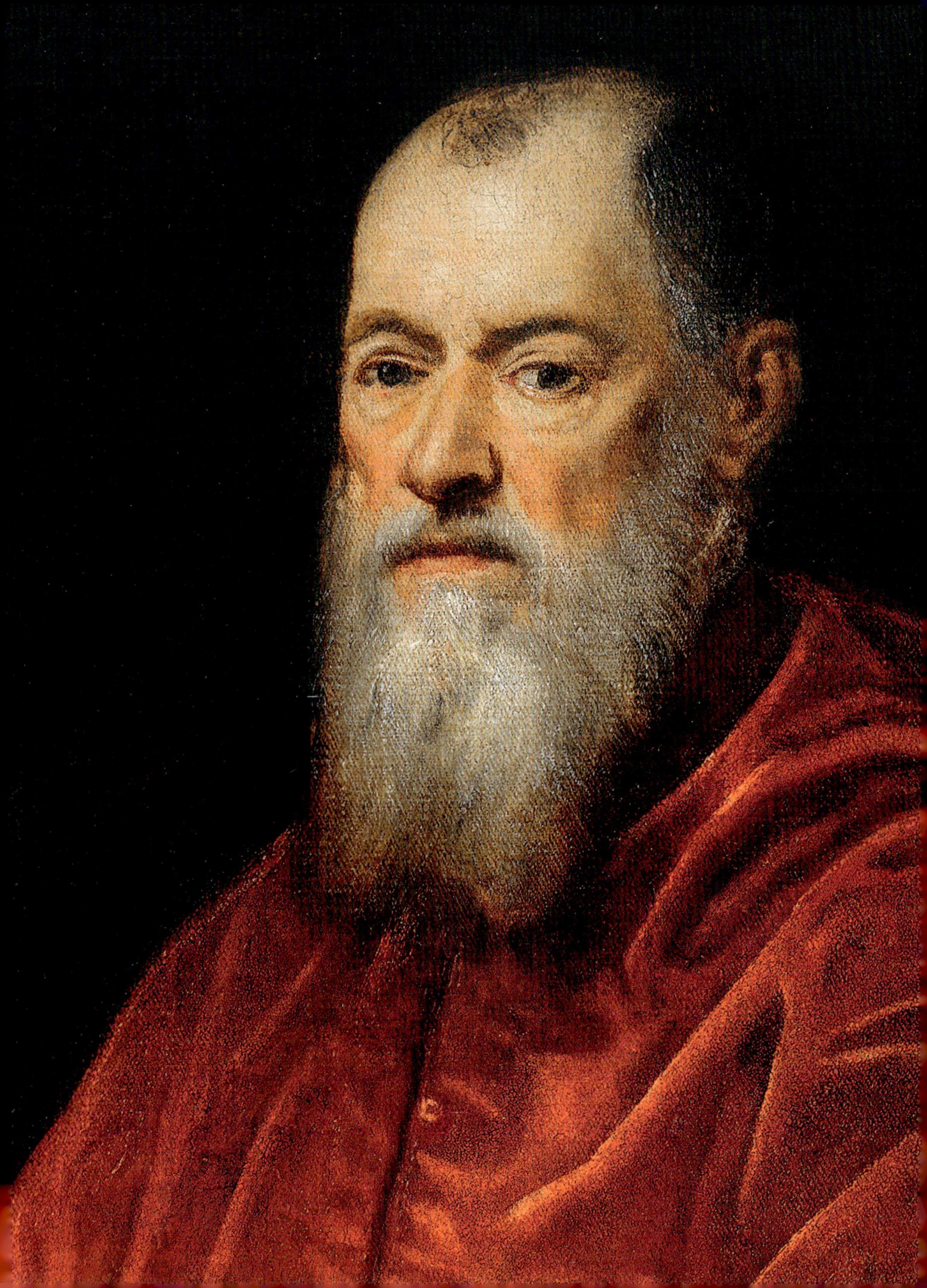

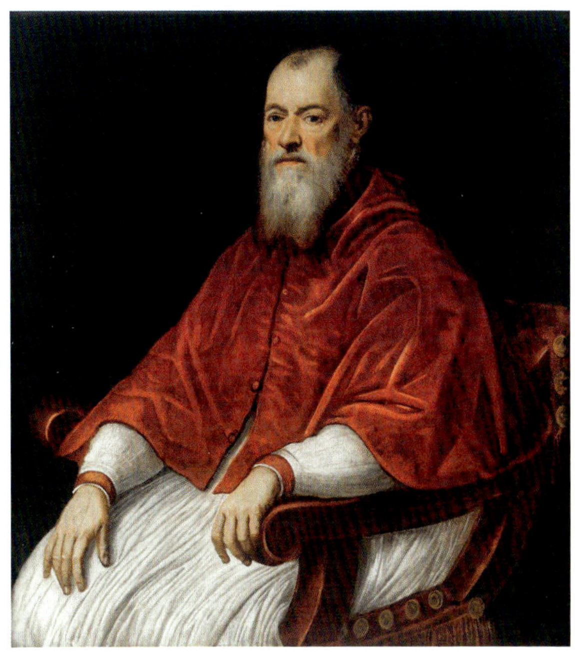

2
Jacopo Tintoretto,
Portrait of Giovanni Grimani,
second half of the sixteenth century
oil on canvas, 115 × 102 cm
Schorr Collection, London

care. Here, the sleeved arms, armrests, and hands are painted summarily, with quick strokes that give a rough indication of the forms and disregard the surface effects, resulting in a lack of relief and, because of that, a slight disproportion of the forearms. The laying-in of the paint in this area does not reveal any discontinuity from the upper part, therefore it does not seem to have been added later or by a different hand. The most logical explanation for this different handling is that the painter concentrated on the bust portrait and filled the available space below with an approximate rendering of elements for which the presence of the sitter was not necessary and could be reworked at a second stage by the artist in his studio. This would confirm the assumption that the portrait was made from life. The completion of the lower part was plausibly aimed at presenting the patron with a full study of the final composition, which the artist finalised by adding the curtain to the right in the background.

The small size of the panel and its modes of execution suggest this was a study for a larger portrait. This assumption is confirmed by the obvious relationship between the painting and a large-size portrait (115 × 102 cm) currently in the Schorr Collection (fig. 2), also displayed in this exhibition, which depicts the same sitter in the painting under examination and is based on the same design.[3] In this larger picture the figure is expanded both in height and in width, to show the curve of the legs under the vestment and bring the left-side hem of the *mozzetta* into full view (whereas this is cropped by the right margin in the smaller portrait). Likewise, the whole expanse of the chair can be seen, including parts of the armrest and backrest that are not visible in the smaller portrait. Given that the two portraits are inextricably intertwined, and that the sitter and historical circumstances of the larger portrait have been thoroughly investigated by other scholars, it is necessary to first discuss the latter to better understand our painting.

The earliest known information on this larger portrait dates from 1828, when George Vivian bought it in Venice from the time-honoured Grimani family. In 1949 it was sold by Colnaghi, London. It was the property of Sir Robert Abdy until 1959, then of Mrs. M. Fitzwilliam until 1980.[4] It was acquired from Christie's, London, in 1980, then back with Colnaghi's and sold in 1982. Rodolfo Pallucchini, who published the painting for the first time in 1983, attributed it to Jacopo Tintoretto.[5] He also identified the sitter with a cardinal and inferred that this had to be a member of the Grimani, since they owned the painting. Pallucchini convincingly argued that, among the patriarchs of the family who lived in the sixteenth century, the one portrayed here must be Giovanni Grimani, given that the plausible dating of the Schorr painting (based on stylistic grounds) from no earlier than the late 1540s, and more probably from around 1560, is incompatible with the biography of the other patriarchs Grimani.[6]

The identification of the sitter of the Schorr painting with Giovanni Grimani, to whom Tintoretto was described as 'most intimate' (*confidentissimo*) in a 1580 letter, rests on solid ground and has never been questioned in the published literature.[7] Nevertheless, it must be noted that there are very few other portraits that can be safely associated with Giovanni to confirm this identification.[8] Among these, a medal in the Museo Correr, Venice, where Giovanni Grimani is portrayed in profile, shows some similarities with the effigies in the panel in private collection and in the Schorr painting: the long and bushy beard, the depression of the glabella, the downturned eyebrow, and the sunken cheeks all seem compatible with the features visible in the two paintings. Grimani's effigy is displayed in another medal in the Civici Musei, Udine, but the rendering of the face is too fuzzy to provide conclusive evidence. Finally, Grimani's likeness appears in a drawing in a seventeenth century manuscript in the Biblioteca Correr, Venice, containing biographies of the Grimani family (cf. p. 27), yet the effigy of Giovanni is depicted so roughly and generically that it proves useless in order to draw any comparison with the painting.[9] Moreover, Pallucchini's reasoning that the portrait must be of one Grimani on account of the painting's provenance, while persuasive, is still conjectural. Finally, in recent years there have emerged various portraits of one same sitter, depicted either half-bust or seated at three-quarter length, who is equally believed to be patriarch Giovanni Grimani.[10] One of these, attributed to Domenico Tintoretto, is owned by the Museo di Palazzo Grimani and is displayed in the present exhibition (cf. p. 41).[11] However, there is an evident discrepancy between the features of the sitter in this set of paintings, on the one hand, and those of the sitter in the Schorr painting and in the panel in private collection, on the other; a discrepancy that can hardly be explained by reference to ageing or illness, as proposed by Firpo.[12] This inconsistency is further accentuated by comparison with the aforementioned Correr medal, with which the effigy in the Museo Grimani painting seems to have only a vague resemblance. Interestingly, the measurements of the painting now in the Museo Grimani (116 × 101 cm) almost coincide with those of the Schorr painting. George Vivian recorded in his notebook two portraits by Tintoretto in the Palazzo Grimani, one depicting the Patriarch of Aquileia, Domenico Grimani, the other portraying an unnamed Cardinal from the same family tree.[13] Because Domenico's likeness, known from various portraits, is entirely different from those of the sitter in the Museo Grimani, the latter cannot be him. However, one *Portrait of Domenico Grimani*, also in the Schorr Collection and attributed to Lorenzo Lotto, has nearly the same measurements (116.8 × 100.3 cm) as the other two portraits examined here.[14] Though of these three paintings only the Schorr portrait believed to depict Giovanni

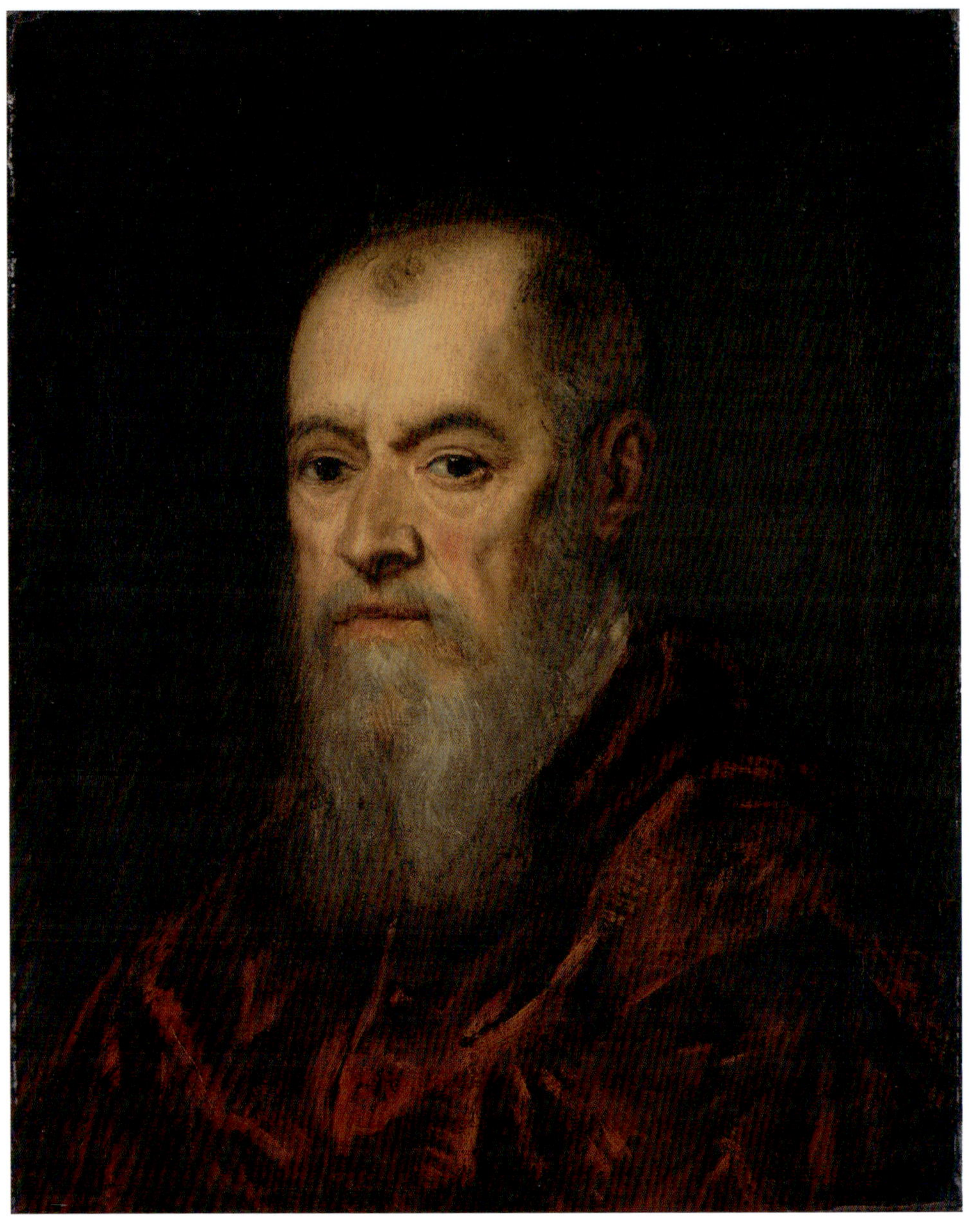

3
Jacopo Tintoretto,
Portrait of Giovanni Grimani,
1555–1580
oil on canvas, 61.5 × 47 cm
Rijksmuseum, Amsterdam, Gift of
Leden van de Vereniging Rembrandt

Grimani is known to come from the Palazzo Grimani, all three could have formed a consistent series conceived for the same setting.

As noted by Firpo, the sitter in the Museo Grimani portrait wears the cardinal's ring.[15] This further complicates his identification, for, as discussed here in the section 'Historical context and dating', Giovanni Grimani was never named cardinal, therefore was not entitled to wear the ring. Nor would he be entitled to wear the cardinal's robes; yet, as argued further below, these would ambiguously blend with the patriarch's robes, thereby making a portrait like the ex-Vivian/Schorr or the one in private collection more acceptable. The only remaining cardinal from the Grimani family who lived in the sixteenth century was the aforementioned Marino, who died in 1546. However, the modes of execution of the Museo Grimani painting and its related versions seem to indicate a date from a period between the late sixteenth and early seventeenth centuries, whereas the argument that they could all derive from an earlier, lost prototype of a Marino Grimani portrait, though possible, would remain speculative.[16] Moreover, his known effigy does not bear any apparent resemblance with that of the sitter in the Museo Grimani portrait.[17] A viable alternative is that the sitter of the Museo Grimani portrait is not from the Grimani family. Considering that portraits of influential statesmen and ecclesiastics were commonly collected and displayed in patricians' houses, it is not impossible that the Grimani owned a portrait of a cardinal who had close ties with them. However, this remains just a hypothesis, with no actual proof. Likewise, the connection between the Museo Grimani portrait and the Grimani family is, at present, more speculative than not.[18] In conclusion, in light of the above considerations, Pallucchini's identification of the ex-Vivian/Schorr painting as a portrait of Giovanni Grimani is still well grounded and provides a valid point of departure for examining the oil on panel version.

Apart from the detail of the curtain and the expansion described above, the design of the painting in private collection corresponds with that of the Schorr portrait. Just the head and facial features have been slightly adjusted, apparently as the natural result of reworking the model. A comparative analysis of the two paintings seems to exclude that the smaller portrait is a copy taken from the larger one. This is suggested by the more vivid rendering, in the portrait on panel, not only of the sitter's gaze, but also of the *mozzetta*. The folds of the red cape are painted with high precision, by means of soft variations of light and shade that faithfully imitate the forms and creases of the fabric. In the Schorr painting, the folds generally follow the pattern of the smaller portrait but are stylised and painted by means of broad, directional strokes that render the highlights as continuous, elongated, and less naturalistic stripes. All this corroborates the impression that the portrait on panel was painted from life, and served as a model for the other painting.

A third picture of the same sitter, similar in size but slightly larger than the panel in private collection (61.5 × 47 cm), is owned by the Rijksmuseum in Amsterdam (fig. 3).[19] The sitter is depicted at half-bust length and wears a darker cape. His features are more similar to those of the sitter in the panel in private collection than of the one in the Schorr version. Both Gronau and Erich von der Bercken put the two versions in direct relation with one another.[20] On the other hand, Pallucchini cautiously intimated that "it is not improbable" ("non è improbabile") that the Amsterdam painting was painted from life and served as a model for the larger portrait.[21] However, since Pallucchini did not mention the version on panel, it seems that his tentative claim rested on the fact that the Amsterdam painting was the only potential model of the Schorr painting known to him. Judging from reproductions of the Amsterdam version, the execution is of good quality but, again, the gaze especially lacks the intensity of the sitter in the panel painting and does not seem to reflect a study from life. In this respect, it should be considered that the rendering of the gaze is possibly the most challenging detail for an artist to reproduce when drawing from life. Moreover, in the Amsterdam portrait, the head and bust have been placed at the centre of the picture in a more stable, but also stiffer, way, as if it had been adjusted to gain compositional balance. All this considered, the Amsterdam version seems to be derived from our painting (or the Schorr one) rather than taken from life.

Against this background, Tintoretto's authorship of the panel in private collection is quite straightforward. Its style and modes of execution point

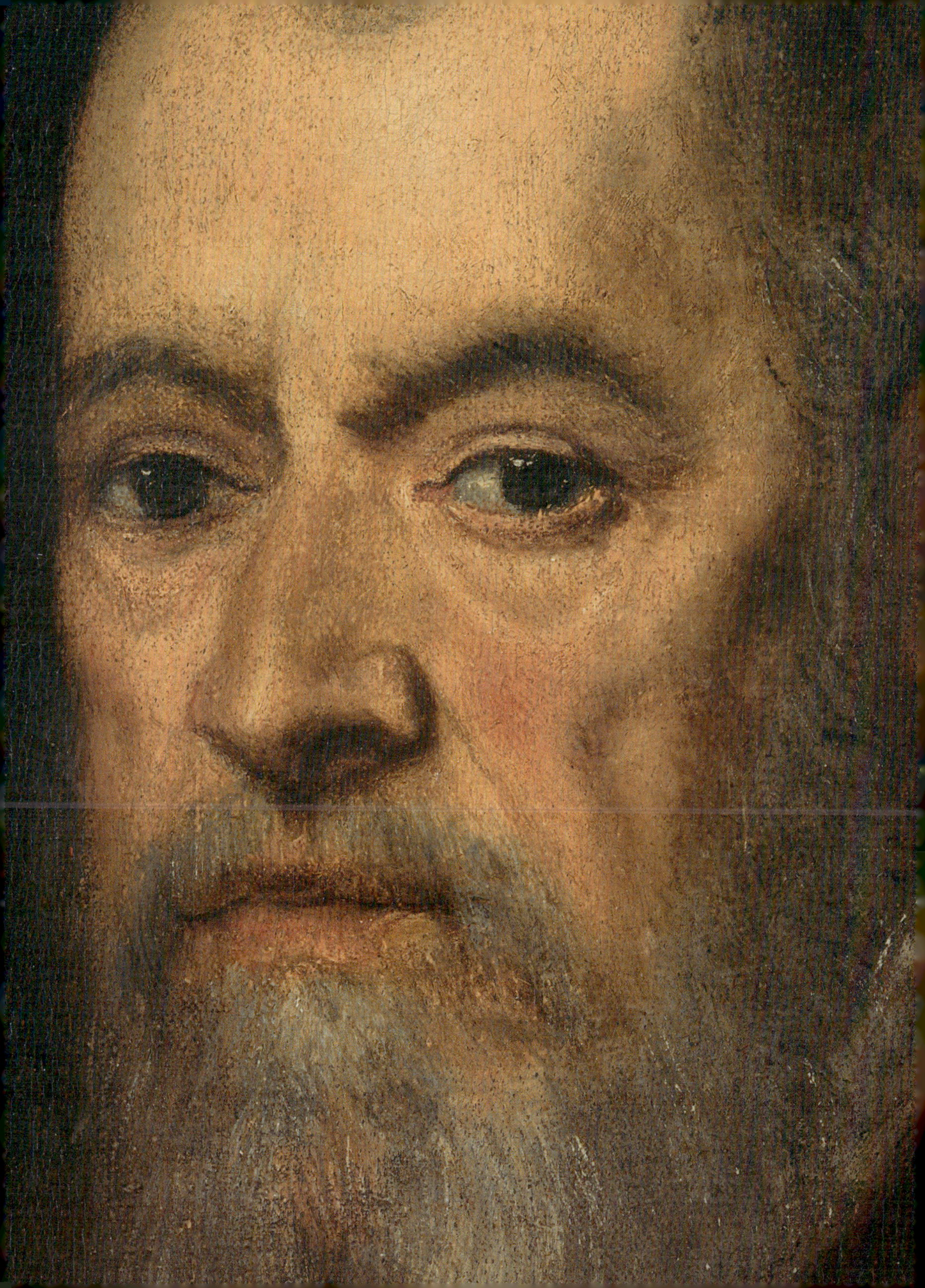

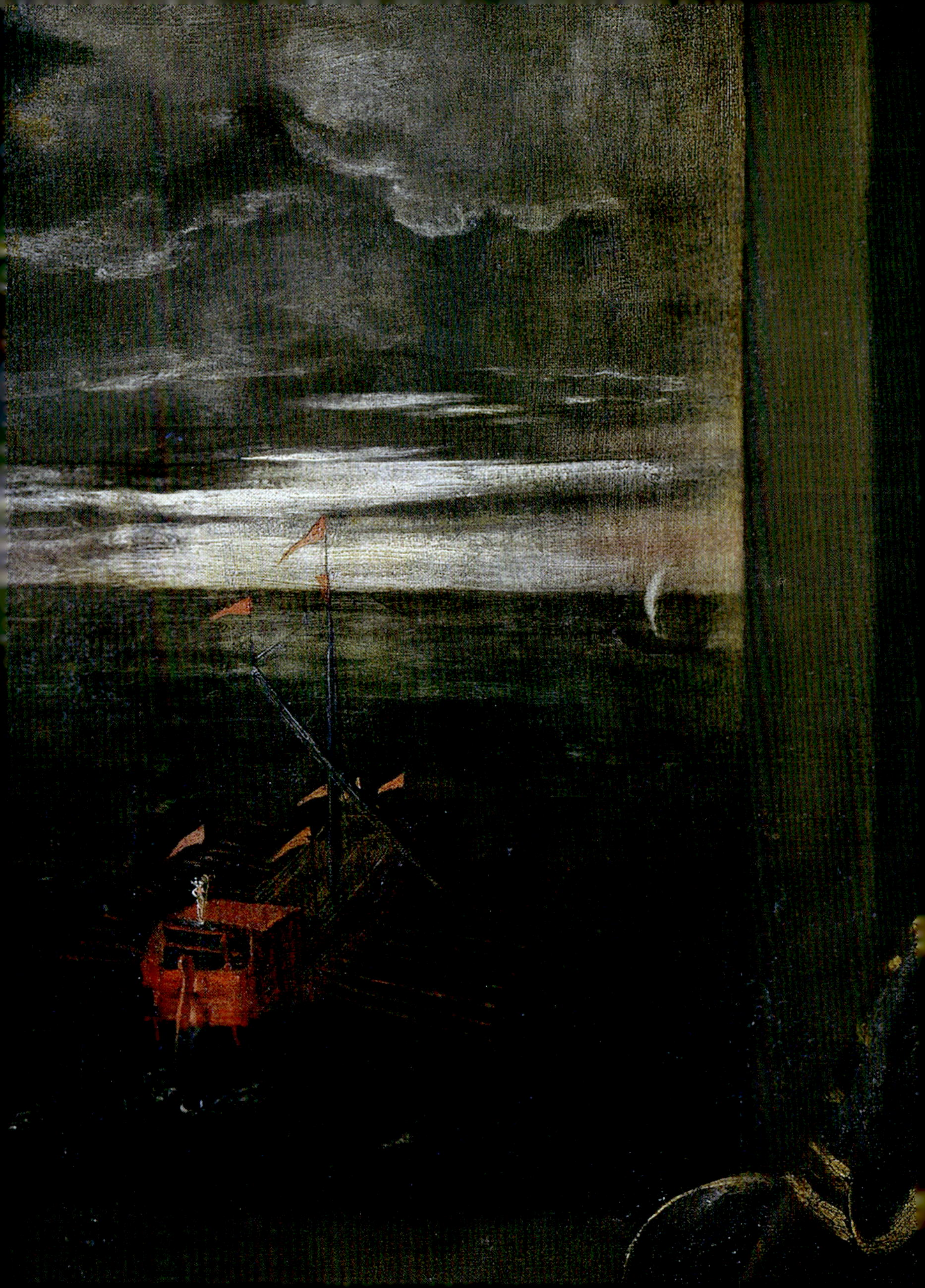

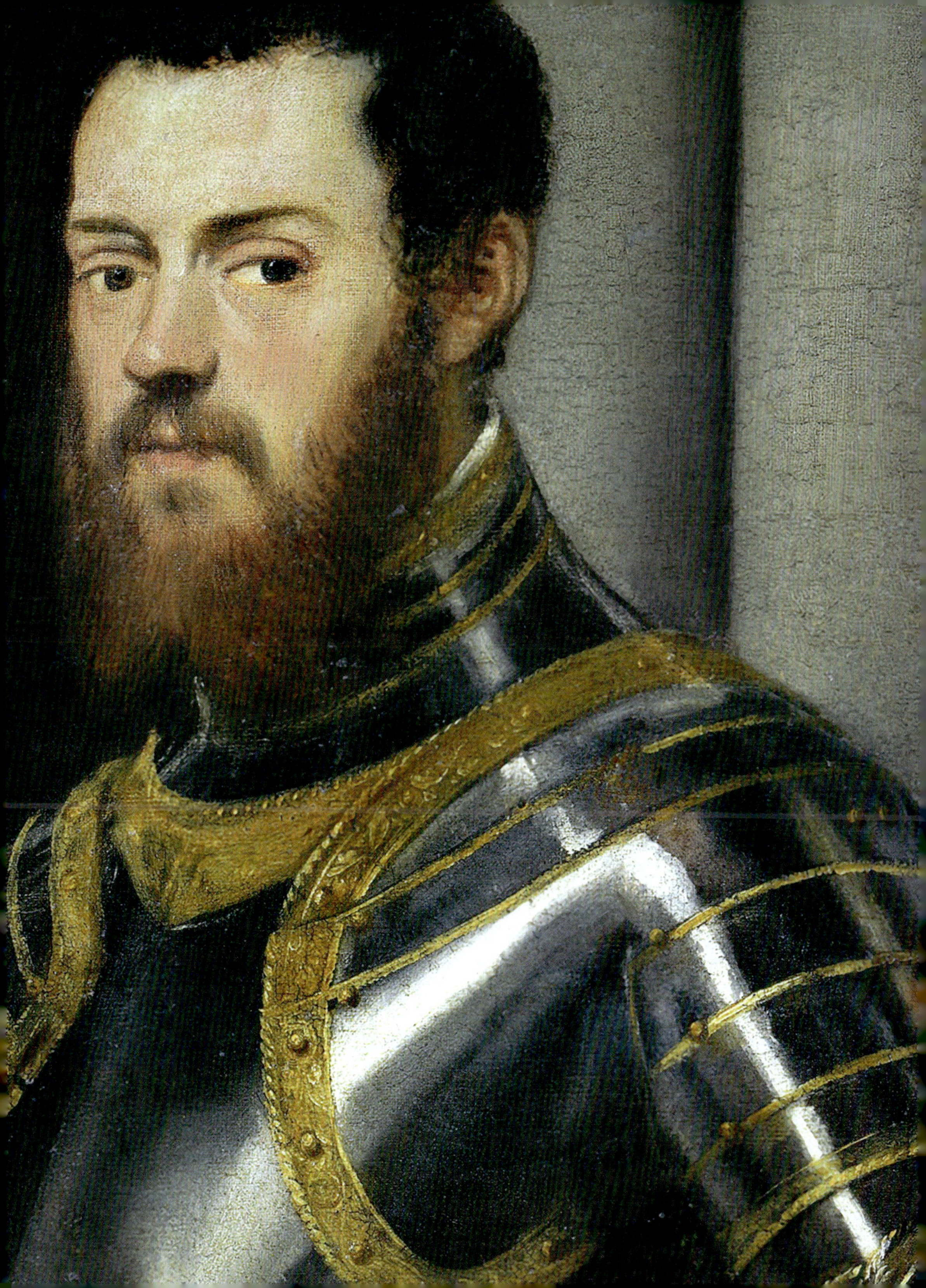

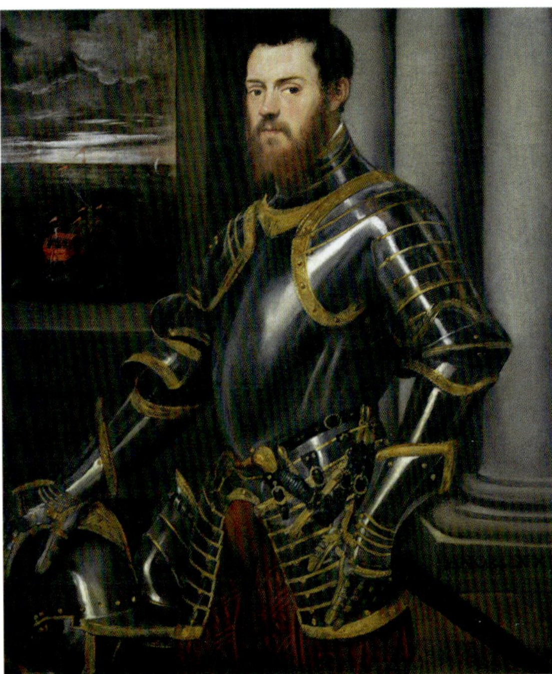

4
Jacopo Tintoretto,
Portrait of a Man in Armour,
ca. 1555–1560
oil on canvas, 115 cm × 99 cm,
Kunsthistorisches Museum, Vienna

unmistakably to the Venetian master. The formal characteristics previously observed in the execution of the sitter's face—the firm line that delineates the contour of the head and runs straight downward downward along the proper right-hand side of the face; the way of drawing and giving relief to the nose, with the pool of light on the tip and a deep shade in and around the nostrils; the sagged cheeks; the various degrees of light to carve the eye sockets; the directness of the gaze—can be compared with some of the best examples of Tintoretto's portraiture. These include: *Portrait of a Thirty-Year Man in Armour* (Kunsthistorisches Museum, Vienna, fig. 4); *Portrait of a Man* (The Metropolitan Museum of Art, New York, fig. 6); *Portrait of Giovanni Paolo Cornaro* (Museum voor Schone Kunsten, Ghent, fig. 5); *Portrait of a Young Man* (Pinacoteca di Brera, Milan, fig. 7); *Portrait of a Man with a White Beard* (Kunsthistorisches Museum, Vienna, fig. 8); and *Portrait of Giovanni Mocenigo* (Staatliche Museen, Gemäldegalerie, Berlin, fig. 9). Moreover, the format and design are consistent with numerous other Tintoretto portraits depicting a seated figure.

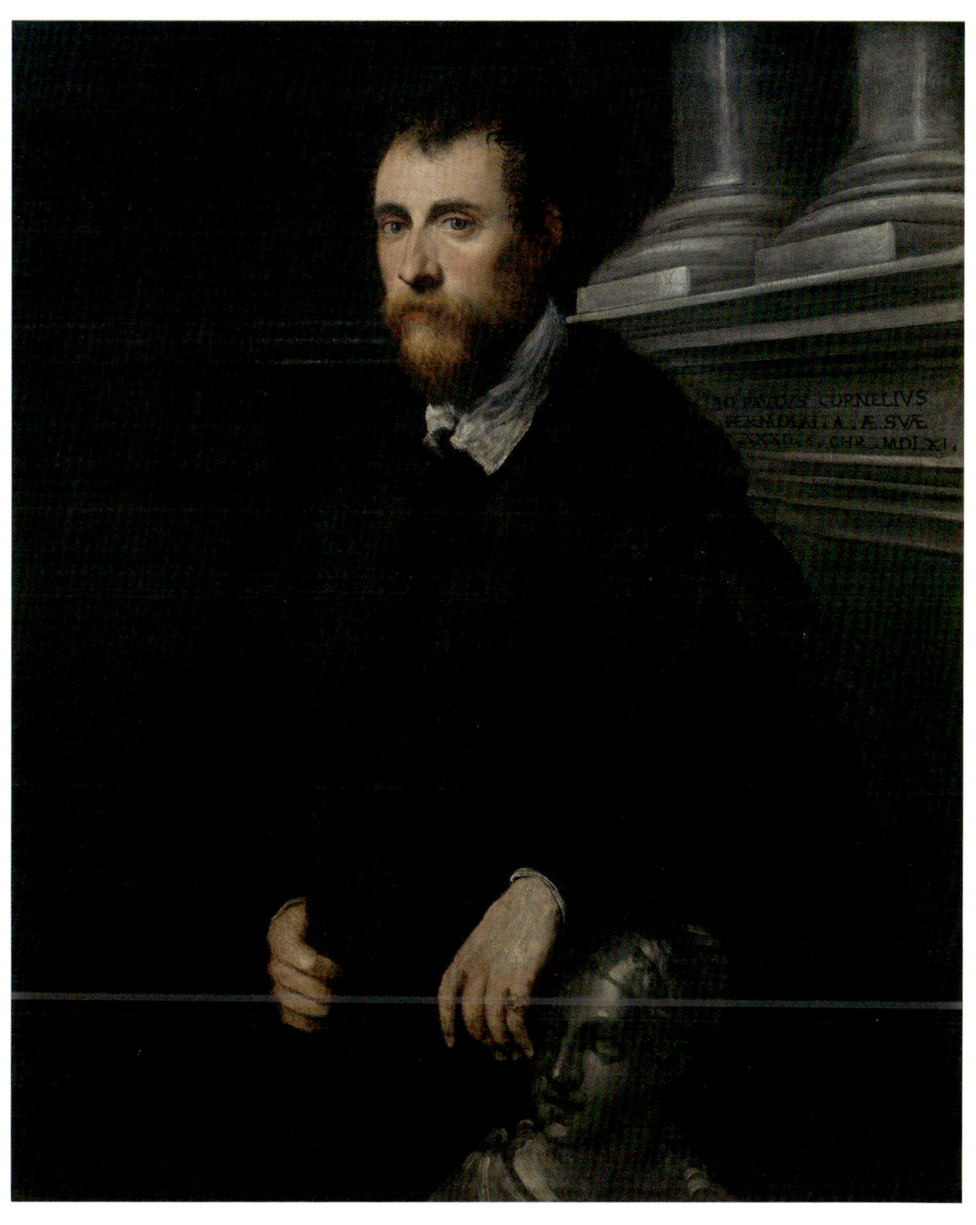

5
Jacopo Tintoretto, *Portrait of
Giovanni Paolo Cornaro*, 1561
oil on canvas, 102 × 81.2 cm
Museum voor Schone Kunsten, Ghent,
bequest Scribe, Fernand Ghent 1913

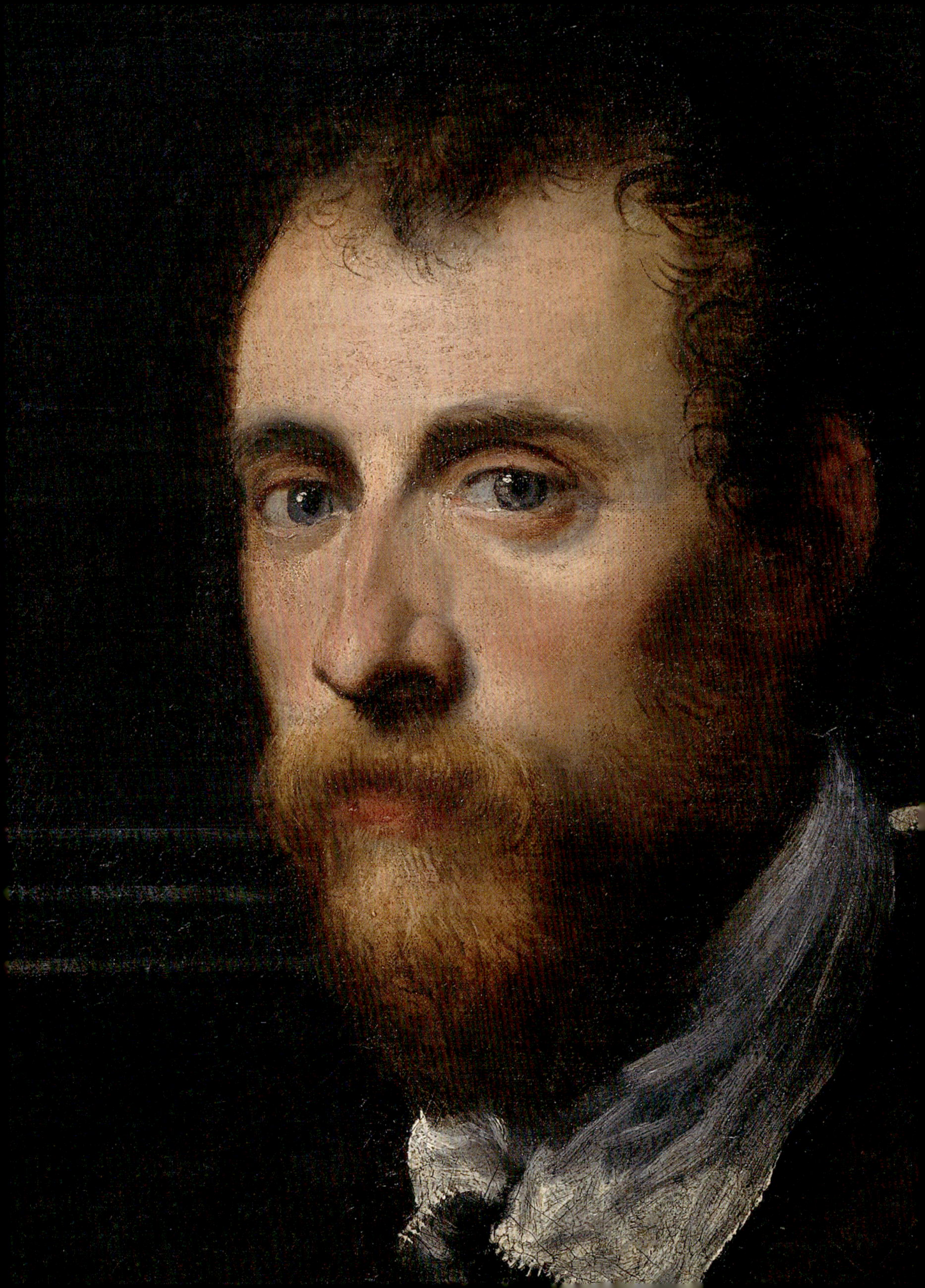

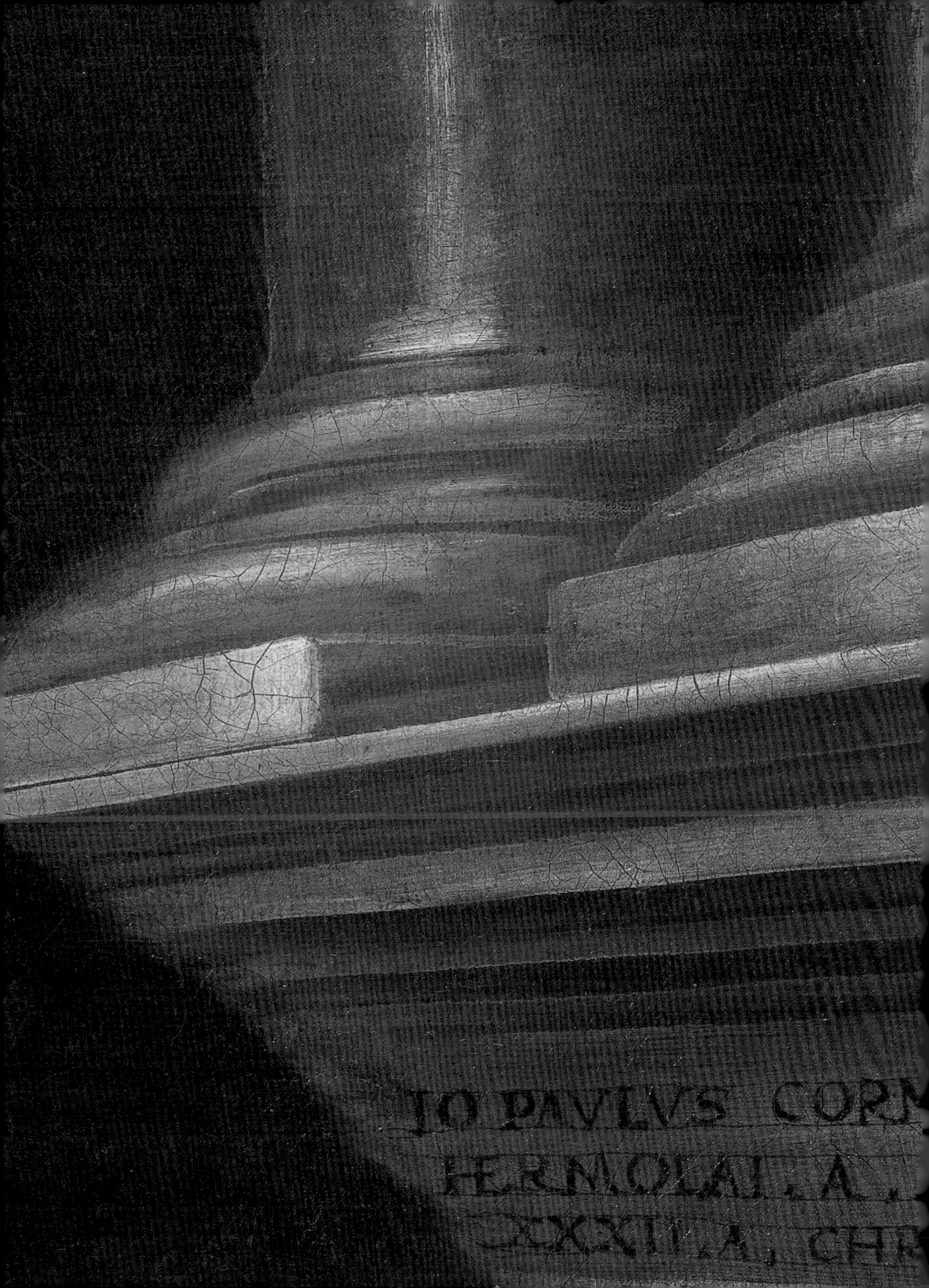
IO PAVLVS COR
ERMOLAI A
XXII A CHR

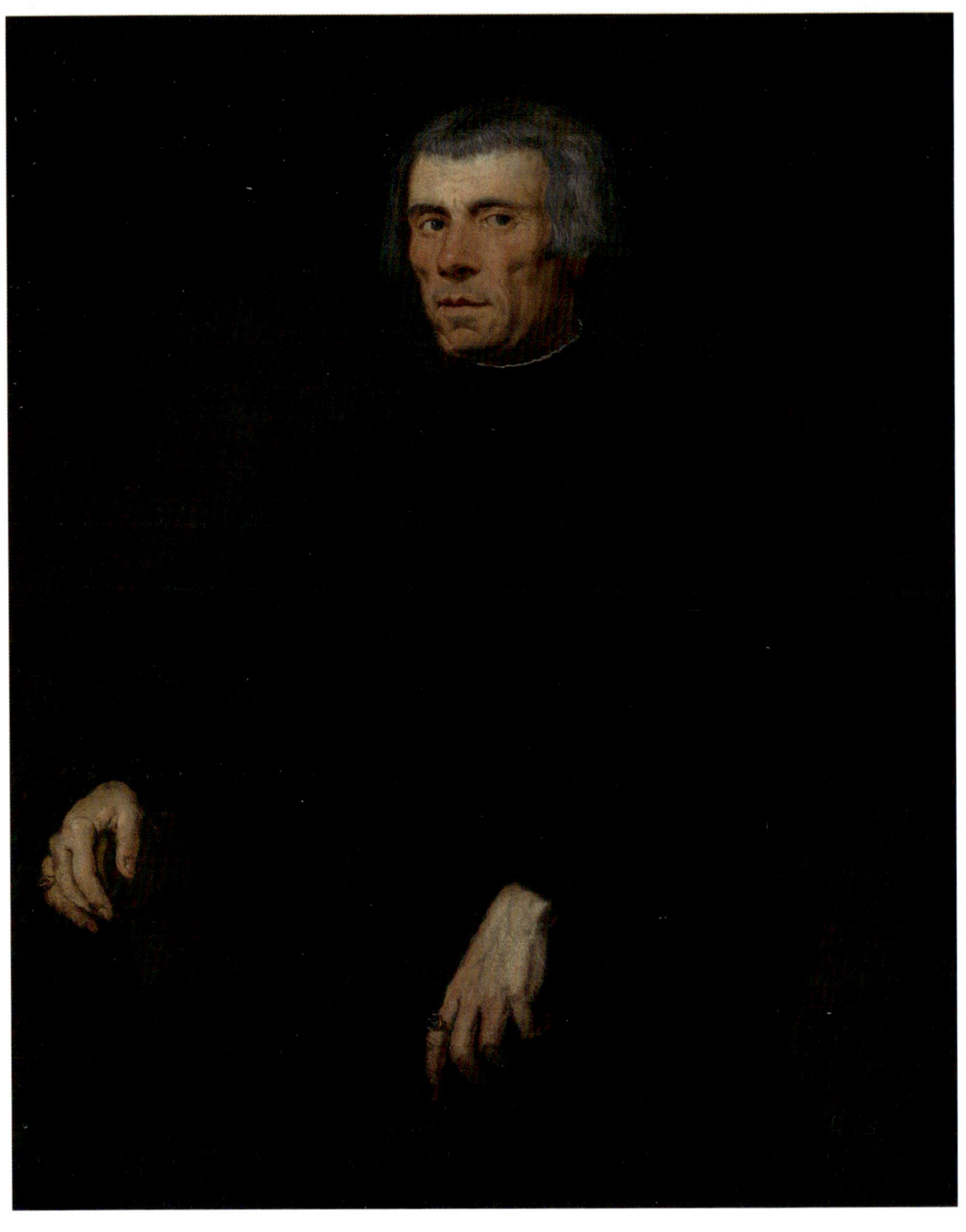

6
Jacopo Tintoretto, *Portrait of a Man,*
ca. 1550
oil on canvas, 112.7 × 88.9 cm
The Metropolitan Museum
Museum of Art, New York,
Gift of George Blumenthal, 1941

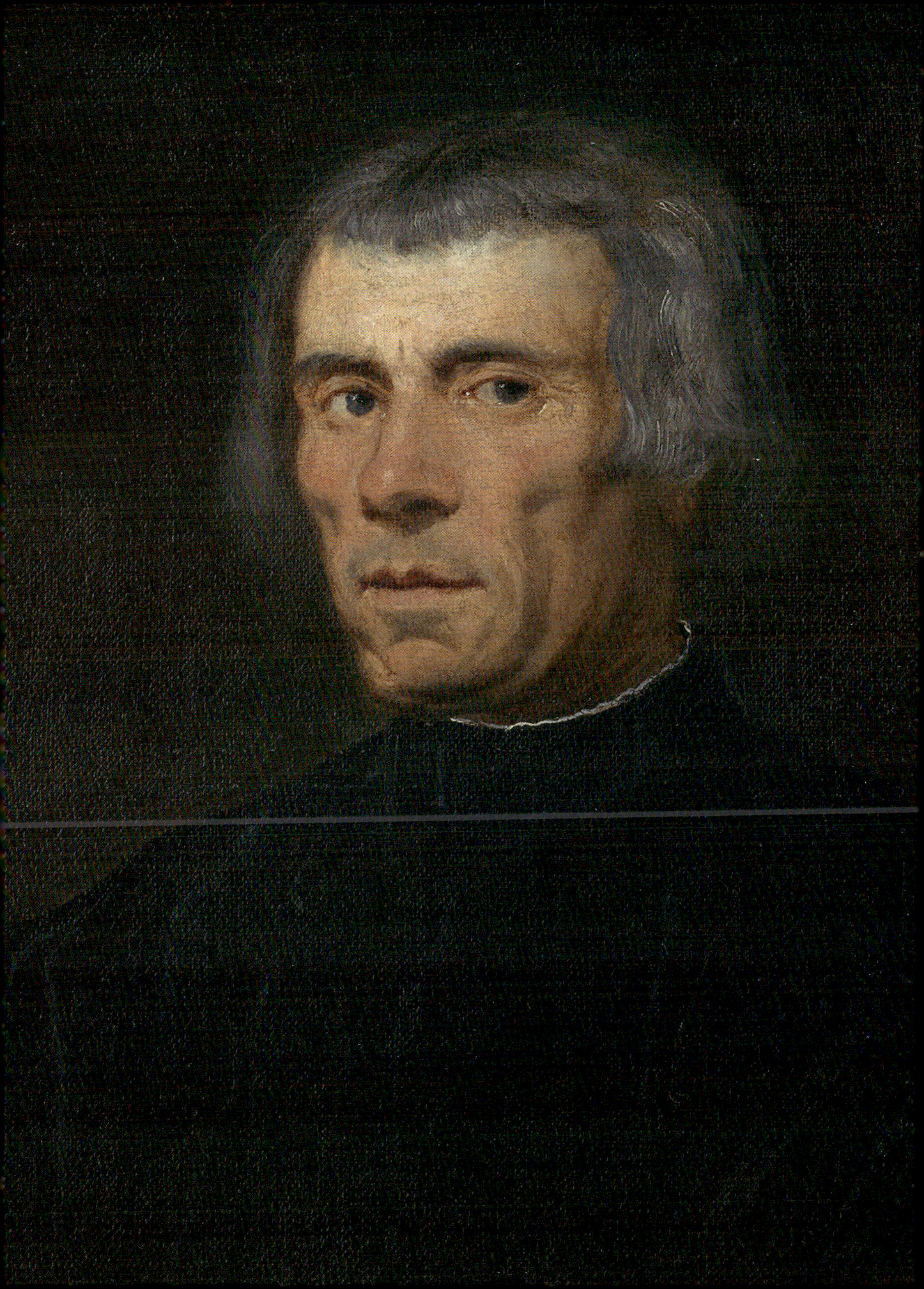

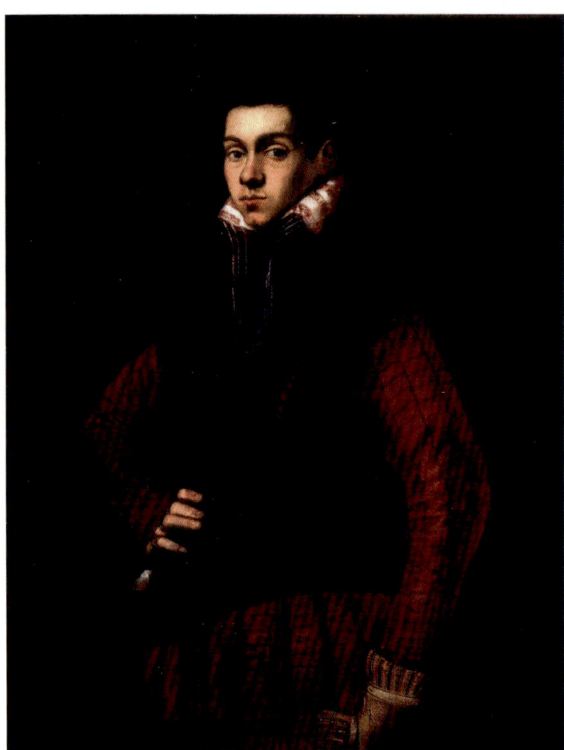

7
Jacopo Tintoretto,
Portrait of a Young Man, ca. 1565
oil on canvas, 115 × 85 cm
Pinacoteca di Brera, Milan

Pallucchini emphasised the "dignified" ("aulico") character of this pattern, which he reconnected with Titian's famed *Portrait of Pope Paul III*, known in various versions (fig. 10). Here the pope is seated on a similar armchair and almost in the same posture as seen in the panel in private collection, just mirrored horizontally, with his right-hand side nearer to us. Tintoretto could indeed have known and drawn on Titian's model, which would be particularly suitable for ennobling the sitter. In any case, the panel in private collection demonstrates a typically less flamboyant and more uncomplicated, but no less moving and engaging, portraiture style, which is a trademark of Tintoretto. Indeed, despite the smaller size and its being a study for a larger picture, this painting stands to comparison with some of Tintoretto's best portraits. Venturi praised the "supreme potency of the modelling in the passionate and angular head, with shiny and alert eyes

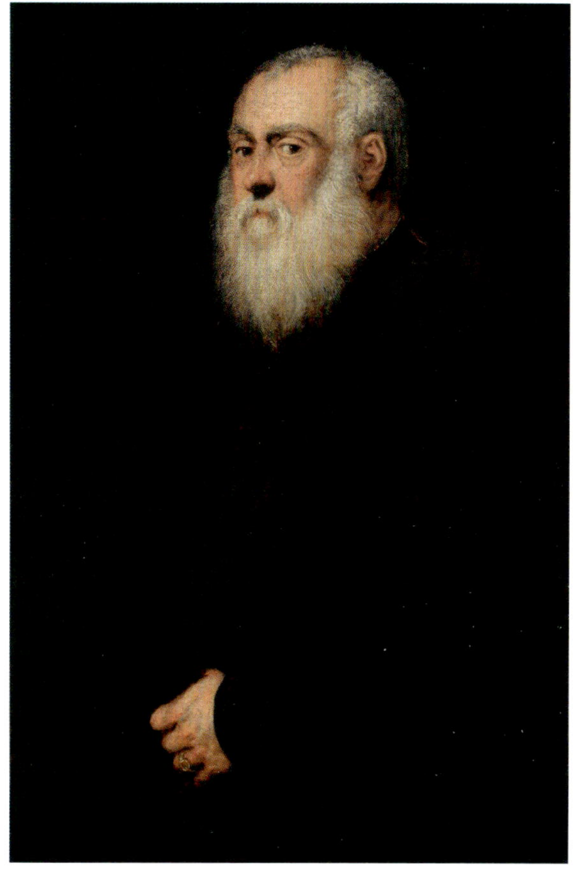

8
Jacopo Tintoretto, *Portrait of a Man
with a White Beard*, ca. 1570
oil on canvas, 92.4 × 59.5 cm
Kunsthistorisches Museum, Vienna

of a steel grey."[22] The quality of the painting can be better appreciated by contrast with the Amsterdam version, which, like the Schorr painting, is also attributed to Jacopo.[23] In comparison with these two, the panel in private collection appears superior in terms of finesse. However, it must be noted that this judgment is based on photo reproductions rather than on direct examination of the Schorr painting.[24] The sitter is imbued with more vigour and lifelikeness, the effect on the viewer is more arresting. Further, when compared with the Schorr portrait, the intensity, precision, and delicacy of paint handling of the panel in private collection stands out against the stylisation of the larger version. Pallucchini noted that the expressiveness of the face in the Schorr painting is perhaps lessened in

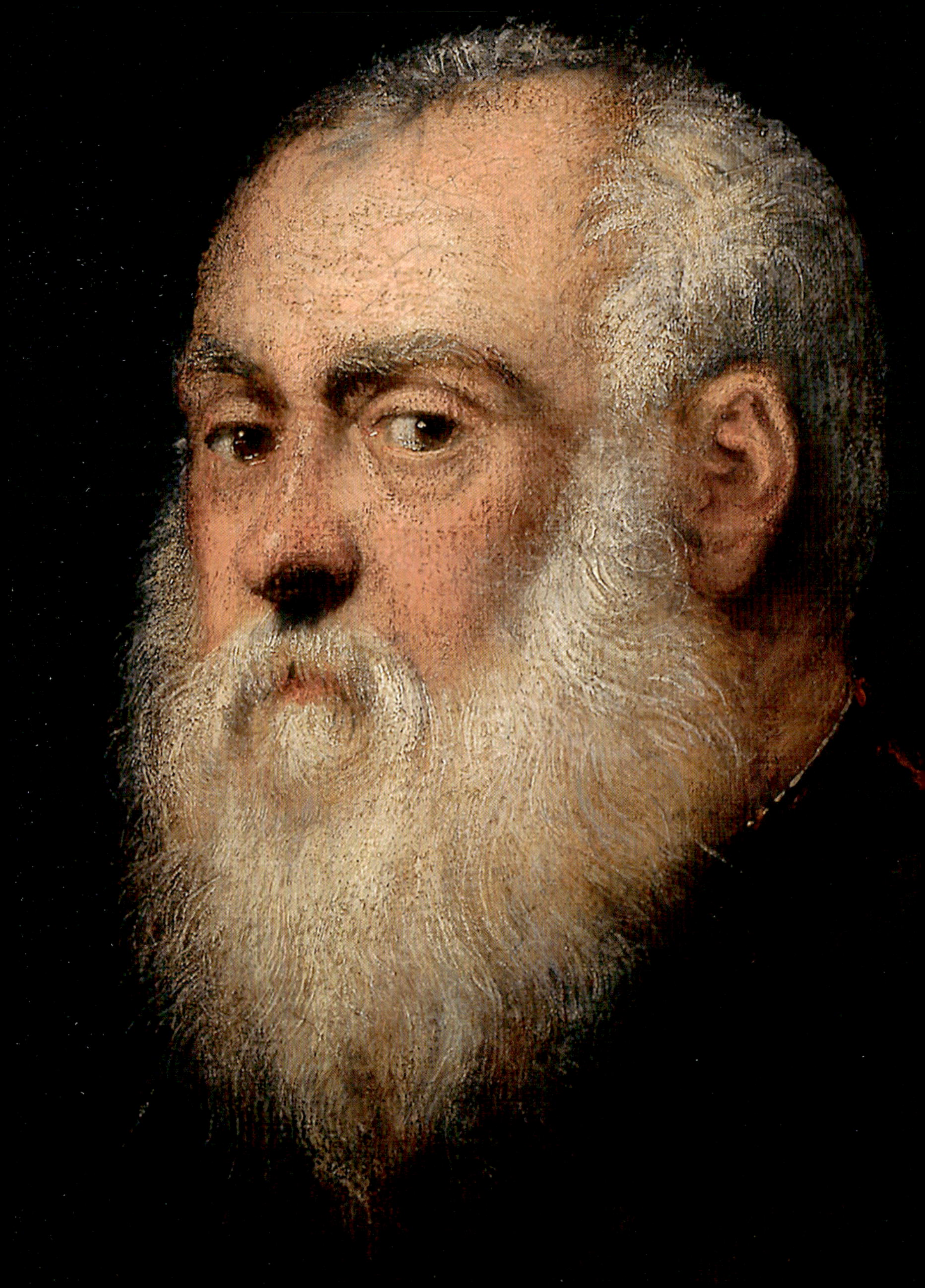

the rest of the figure. Conversely, in the panel version the paint handling does not lose its vibrancy in the area of the red *mozzetta*. As previously argued, the more rapid, less careful execution in the lower section seems to reflect the artist's need to bring to completion the design and present it to the patron. The painting is indeed a rare example of a small-size study portrait by Tintoretto and, even more notably, painted on panel instead of canvas.

Historical context and dating

The dating and context of production of the painting is inevitably dependent on the proposed identification of the sitter as Giovanni Grimani. Therefore, to follow up on this identification, an examination of Grimani's vicissitudes in relation to the ecclesiastical office referred to in the portrait and the historical circumstances in which the latter could have been commissioned is essential. The following discussion is based especially on Pio Paschini's reconstruction of Grimani's biography.[25]

Giovanni Grimani was handed the title of Patriarch of Aquileia by his brother Marino in January 1545. Exactly one year later, an accusation of heresy was levelled against Giovanni by another prelate, Dionisio Zanettini, bishop of Mylopotamos and Chersonesos, who, in 1547, reiterated the charge. On that occasion, the accuser bitterly commented that Grimani pretended to behave like a cardinal. Indeed, Grimani's following attempts to free himself from these allegations and from the grip of the Inquisition mingled with a long-drawn campaign for his election to cardinal. This would cost him years of tribulations and came to nothing, despite the backing (and pressure) of the Republic of Venice, which sought, by upholding Grimani, "to maintain a de facto territorial church in order to harvest the church's wealth".[26] An extra motivation for pursuing the cardinalate was that this would be instrumental in preserving Gromani's office as patriarch. To bequeath the patriarchate from one another, the Grimani had exploited an ecclesiastical procedure called *resignatio cum regressu*, by means of which a prelate could give up a benifice to someone else but hold the right to regain it under certain circumstances,

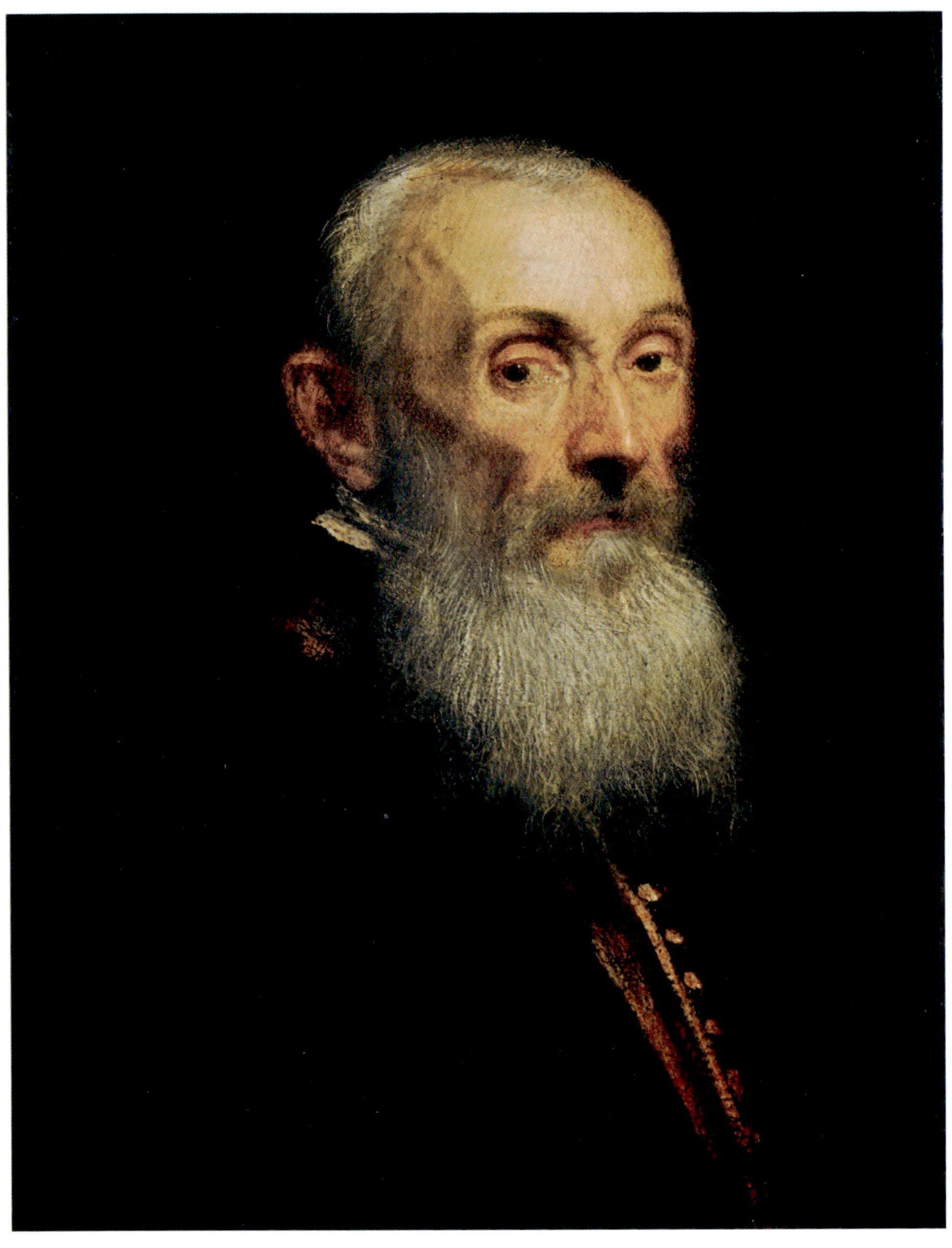

9
Jacopo Tintoretto, *Portrait of
Giovanni Mocenigo*, ca. 1580
oil on canvas, 58.5 × 44.5 cm
Staatliche Museen, Gemaldegalerie,
Berlin

e.g. the death of the temporary beneficiary. However, in the mid 1540s this practice had been declared illegal and allowed only to cardinals;[27] it therefore became of strategic importance that Grimani obtained the cardinalate in order to maintain his right, especially after the Republic asked him to elect a successor so as not to lose the Venetian hegemony over the patriarchate.

Following Pallucchini, the Schorr portrait has been legitimately interpreted against this context. As summarised by Benjamin Paul: "We may consider Tintoretto's portrait as part of Grimani's strategy to promulgate his alleged secret cardinalship . . . . By continuously fashioning himself a cardinal, both in his public appearances with the help of the Serenissima but also in paintings, Grimani aimed at establishing himself in the public consciousness as effectively occupying the office".[28] If this reading is correct, then the date of the Schorr painting should fit the chronology of Grimani's attempts to become cardinal, which were interwoven with his endeavours to be acquitted from the charge of heresy. A summary of the key events is therefore necessary.

Following the accusations, Grimani went to Rome in 1550 to advocate his cause before Pope Julius III. In 1552 the patriarch underwent a formal *purgazione* (a demonstration of innocence), and in 1554 the Republic put forward a formal request to the papal nuncio in Venice that Grimani be appointed cardinal. Negotiations were still ongoing in 1555–1556, but the new elected Pope Paul IV (1555–1559) was not favourable to Grimani. With the following pope, Pius IV (1559–1565), the Venetians tried again to negotiate, and in 1560 there were rumours that Grimani would have been soon nominated. In February 1561 the Republic put pressure on the pope through the Venetian ambassador in Rome, Marcantonio Da Mula, to include Grimani in the selection of new cardinals to be soon elected. Ironically, the ambassador Da Mula was appointed, not Grimani. In passing, it should be noted that a recently published portrait (fig. 11), attributed to Tintoretto, depicts Da Mula seated in an armchair and dressed as a cardinal, complete with the hat, which somehow resonates with the Schorr portrait of Grimani.[29] What the Republic was able to obtain, just few days after the missed election, was Pius IV's pledge to have Grimani soon elected only with the votes of those cardinals who had approved of his nomination. However, while the Venetian state would later try to leverage the pope's word to make a case for Grimani's appointment, this promise was never fulfilled. On the contrary, in the following months Grimani was hit by a new wave of accusations that compelled the pope to call for trial. It was only in the late summer of 1563 that Grimani was judged at the Council of Trent by a specially formed jury and eventually absolved of any charge of heresy (September 1563). The acquittal reinvigorated Grimani's hopes and, building on the momentum, the Republic sent Pius IV a new request. This was, once more, unsuccessful. Later in 1565, a new batch of cardinals was named, yet Grimani was not among them. At the end of the same year, Pius IV died and was succeeded by Pius V (1566–1572), who was notoriously hostile to Grimani. For this reason, the Republic held off making further requests concerning Grimani's cardinalate until a new pope was elected. But, when this happened, in the autumn of 1572, Gregory XIII (1572–1585) sent a definitive rejection that settled the question once and for all.

All this considered, the time span during which Grimani could have commissioned a portrait to promote himself would range from around 1546, when he was said to behave as if he were a cardinal, and 1572, when his campaign came to an end. Within this time frame, the periods when he and the Republic were probably in a stronger position to lay claim to his election were: 1552–1554 (between the *purgazione* and the first request sent to the pope by the Republic); 1560–1561 (between Pius IV's election and pledge to have Grimani nominated); and 1563–1565 (after Grimani's acquittal and the new batch of cardinals). After 1565 Grimani's chances to become cardinal waned considerably, and it is unlikely that he would resort to a portrait to reinforce his claim. The Schorr painting was dated to around 1560 by Pallucchini on stylistic grounds;[30] this hypothesis has never been challenged. Building on that, Firpo has suggested that the portrait was painted either near the election of cardinals in February 1561, in which Grimani hoped to be nominated, or in 1563, after Grimani's trial.[31]

Any attempt to date the panel in private collection must consider the possible time distance that separates it from the Schorr painting. In that

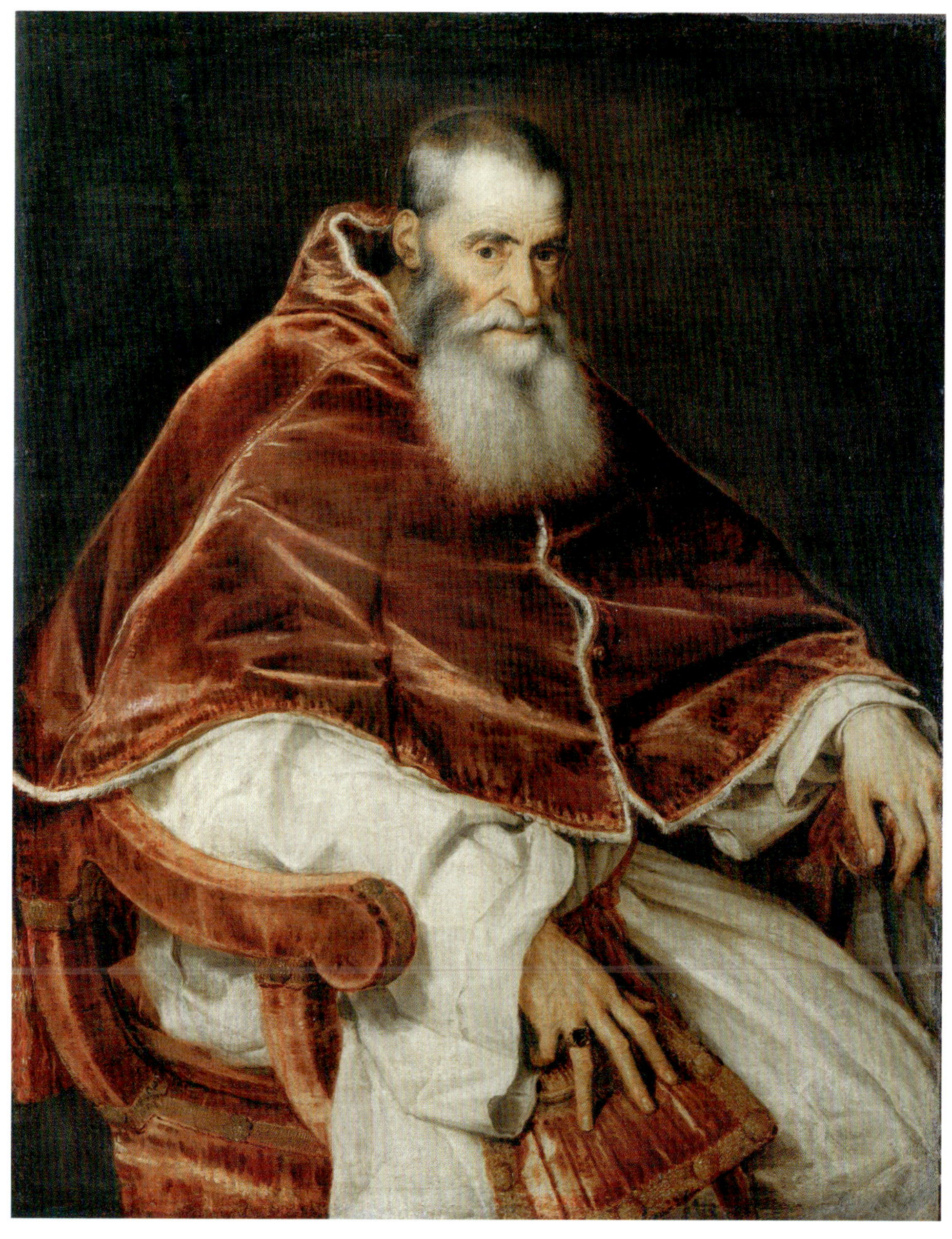

10
Titian, *Portrait of Pope Paul III*, 1543
oil on canvas, 113.7 × 88.8 cm
Museo Nazionale
di Capodimonte, Naples

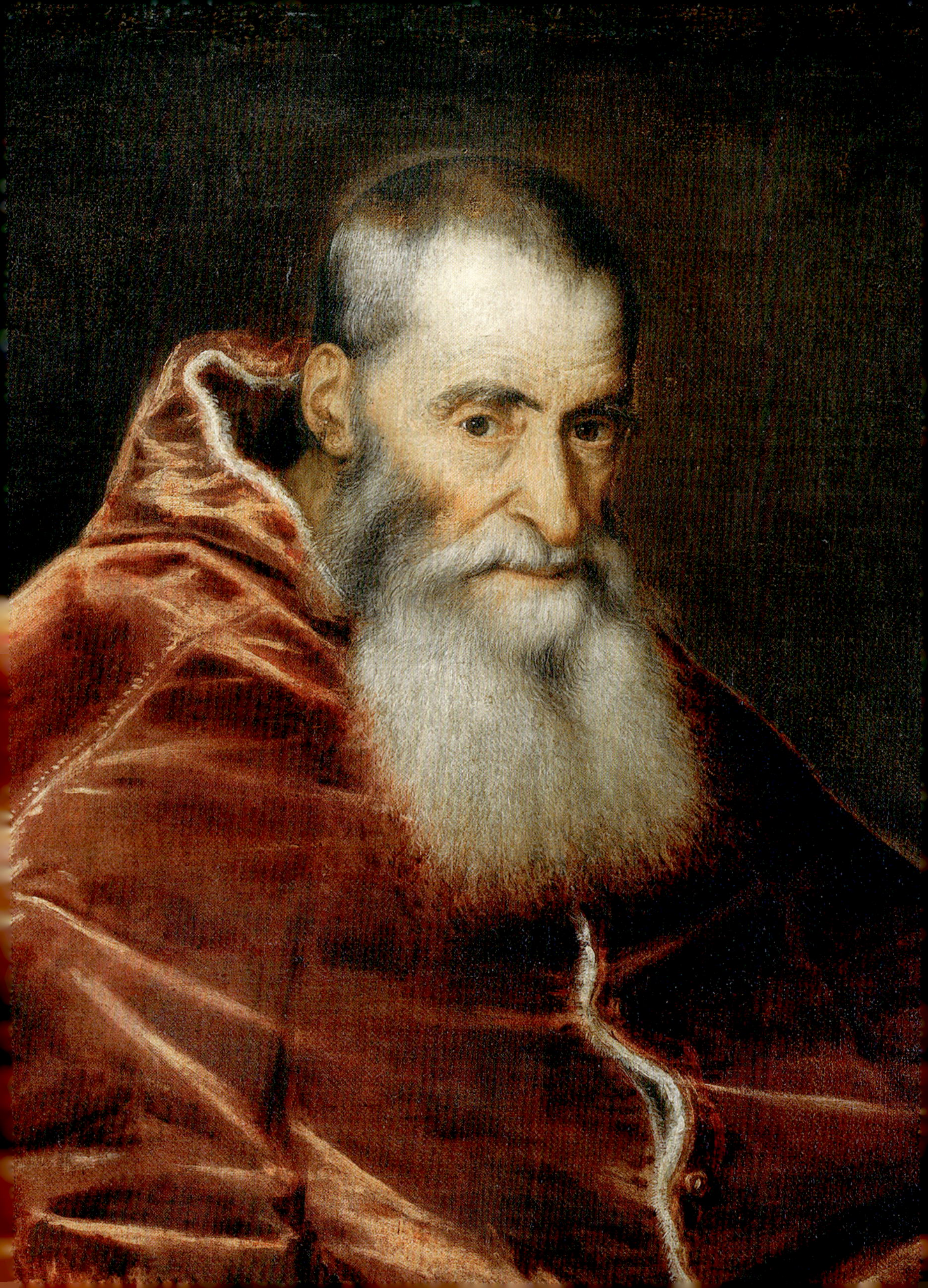

respect, the sitter's age must be taken into account with all the due caveats, for paintings are not photographs, and guessing someone's age even from a photograph proves tricky. Judging from reproductions, the sitter in the Schorr portrait looks slightly older than in the panel in private collection. Gronau believed that in the Amsterdam version the sitter is ten to fifteen years older than in the panel painting. Gronau, however, ignored that the latter was a preparatory study for the Schorr portrait. It is difficult to envisage that a presentation study as accomplished as the latter remained unused for such a long time, especially if the making of the portrait was motivated by Grimani's self-promotion needs. Still, given the ups and downs that the Grimani campaign underwent, it is not implausible that the project was paused and later resumed. All this considered, it is legitimate to assume that the two paintings were executed within a relatively narrow span of time, which may range from few weeks or months to a couple of years, and that the apparent differences in relation to the sitter's age are the result of the artist's reworking of the original model rather than of the actual ageing of the patron.

In fact, the sitter's age in our painting is difficult to pin down, especially because the grey hair seems to contrast with the spirited look in his eyes. When considered against Grimani's biography, the problem becomes even more complicated. According to ancient genealogists, Grimani was born in July 1506.[32] Therefore, he would be nearly 39 years old when he became patriarch, 46 when he made his *purgazione*, 57 when he was judged at the Council of Trent, and 59 when Gregory XIII was elected. In the panel in private collection, he may look closer to his 60; nevertheless, considering the life expectations of the time and conceding that the sitter might look to us older than he actually was, an age between 50 and 55 would still be possible. On the other hand, Pio Paschini suggested that Grimani's real birthdate was around 1500, which, if confirmed, would allow us to better accommodate the apparent age of the sitter in the panel in private collection and the chronology of the campaign for Grimani's cardinalate.[33] Given these uncertainties, the problem of the sitter's age remains open.

Another factor to be considered is the different colour of the *mozzetta* in the three versions of the Grimani portrait.[34] Firpo has observed that the patriarchs of Aquileia were entitled to wear the cardinal red cape.[35] According to Firpo, however, the *mozzetta* worn by patriarchs was of a more faded red than the typical cardinal's *porpora* colour. In his view, therefore, the Schorr painting would play on the ambiguity of the red colour to propound Grimani's right to the cardinalate without crossing a line. Firpo's argument, though, is confusing, since he does not clarify how the different colour gradations in the various paintings he examines must be interpreted. The shades of red in the Schorr painting vary between crimson and cardinal, which does not seem to tally with the faded red Firpo considers distinctive of the patriarchs of Aquileia. Even more puzzling is Firpo's statement that in the Amsterdam version the sitter wears the purple/violet bishop cape, whereas this is of a dark (rosewood) red.[36] In any case, there is no doubt that the panel in private collection depicts a cardinal cape, since it is of a burgundy red that can be seen in a number of cardinal portraits. What is startling is that the *mozzetta* is apparently painted from life, which poses a practical issue, since Grimani, not being named cardinal, was never bestowed upon a cape like the one shown in the picture. In fact, for some reasons he never even received the pallium of patriarch.[37] A plausible hypothesis, however, is that, while sitting before Tintoretto, he worn either his uncle Domenico's or brother Marino's cape. Be that as it may, the *mozzetta* signals that this portrait dates from a time when Grimani was laying claim to the title of cardinal, though. The absence of other distinctive insignia of cardinalate such as the ring and biretta may be indicative of a cautious strategy on the part of the sitter in promoting his image, which would reflect the controversial circumstances previously described, thus further supporting his identification as the sitter of the panel in private collection and Schorr portrait.[38]

Venturi, Biermann and Gronau generally referred the panel in private collection to Tintoretto's early period, without further specification. Subsequently, by combining this evaluation with Gronau's abovementioned observation on the sitter's age, Bercken dated the Amsterdam version to 1565, implying that the portrait on panel should date from 1550–1555. In broad terms, this wide chronological range between early 1550s and early 1560s fits Tintoretto's oeuvre. For the evocativeness of the surface

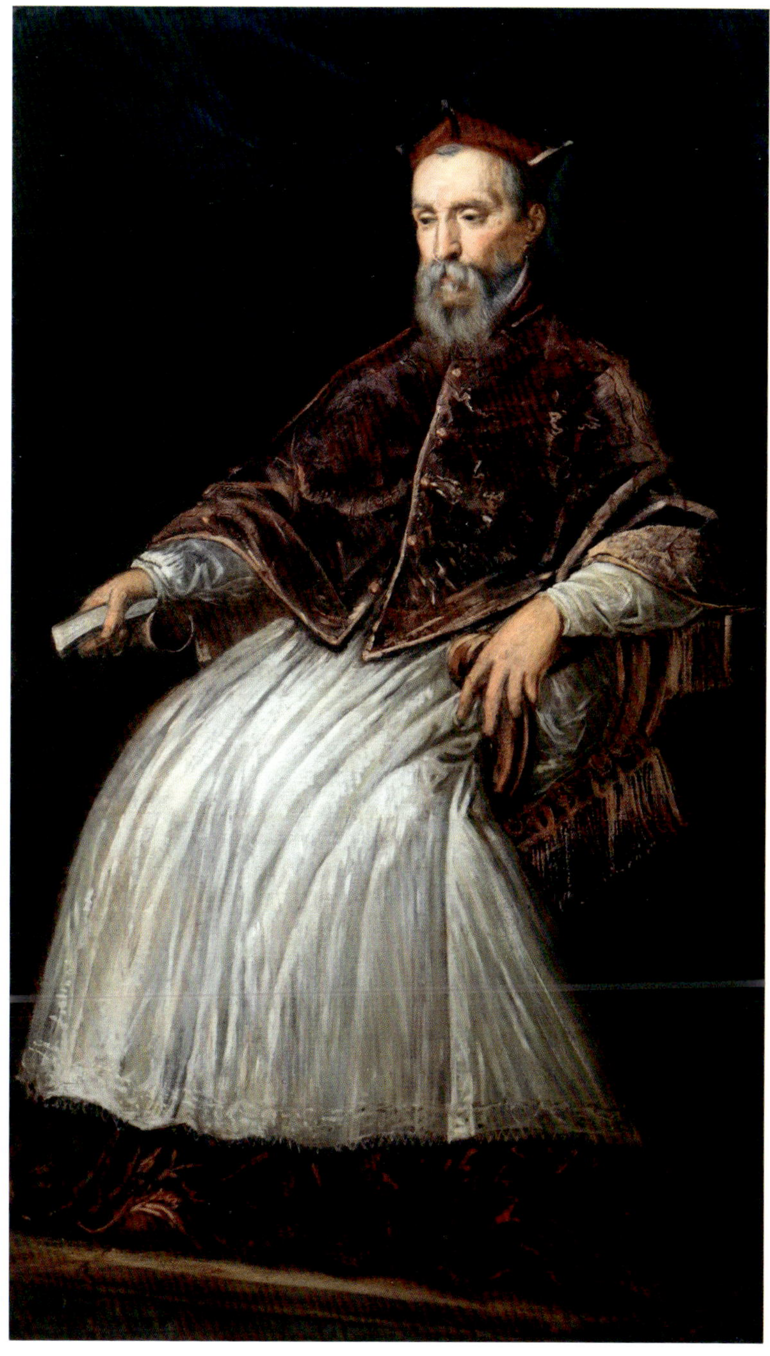

11
Jacopo Tintoretto (attr.), *Portrait
of Cardinal Marcantonio Da Mula*
ca. 1562–1563
oil on canvas, 187 × 103 cm
Private Collection

effects, the sitter's posture, the construction of the head, and the directness of the gaze, the portrait on panel can be likened to the aforementioned *Portrait of a Thirty-Year Man in Armour*, which is commonly dated around 1555–1560. Other similarities, noted above, make it compatible with the *Portrait of Giovanni Paolo Cornaro*, which bears the date 1561 and therefore constitutes a fundamental point in the chronology of Tintoretto's portraiture. All this considered, if the identification of the sitter with Grimani is accepted, the date of the painting can be plausibly situated between 1554 and 1563, thus reconciling all the main chronological indicators considered here. Any further specification is not possible based on the evidence currently available.

Conclusion

The significance of the painting presented here lies both in its outstanding quality and, should the identity of the sitter be confirmed, historical importance. Aside from being a rare, finely executed example of a Tintoretto study portrait, it may represent a remarkable piece of biographical evidence concerning a prominent political figure and art patron in sixteenth century Venice. Further, considering that the Grimani affair was at the centre of the tense relationships between Venice and Rome, the portrait may be considered more broadly as a testimony to a key moment in the history of the Republic of Venice. Finally, it stands out as an extraordinary embodiment of how portraiture in the Renaissance and early modern period was widely exploited by the ruling class as an instrument to promote their public image and support their political agendas.

1 Venturi 1927; Biermann 1927.
2 Gronau 1929.
3 Wright 2014, vol. I, pp. 242–43, no. 385; vol. 2, p. 30. The measurements of the canvas provided by Wright differ slightly from those indicated in Pallucchini 1983: 116.3 × 102.8 cm.
4 Wright 2014, vol. 1, p. 242.
5 Pallucchini 1983.
6 For biographical information on Giovanni and the other Grimani involved here, see the Introduction to this volume by Valeria Finocchi.
7 See Firpo 2010; Wright 2014; Paul 2018; Ferrari 2021. The familiarity between Giovanni and Tintoretto was stresses by Pallucchini 1983, p. 185. For the 1580 letter, see Paschini 1956, p. 855; and, for a full transcription, Paul 2018, p. 39, App. II, no. 5.
8 On this topic, see Valeria Finocchi's Introduction to the present volume.
9 Foscari, Tafuri 1983, pl. 85.
10 Firpo 2010, fig. 47, pls. 35, 38. The identification was accepted by Lionello Puppi: Puppi 2007, pp. 422–23, no. 118.
11 Venetian Heritage 2020; see Christie's 2004; Wright 2014, vol. I, p. 242, "Related Paintings," no. 1; Lempertz 2017.
12 Firpo 2010, p. 160.
13 Wright 2014, vol. I, p. 242, "History".
14 Wright 2014, vol. I, pp. 159–60, no. 217.
15 Firpo 2010, p. 160.
16 Interestingly, Firpo 2010, p. 160, followed by Puppi 2007, p. 422, believes the Museo Grimani portrait and its cognate versions derive from the Schorr painting identified as the portrait of Giovanni Grimani.
17 See Hochmann 2014, fig. 1.
18 The problem is further examined in this volume by Francesco Trentini, who in his essay takes into consideration the possibility that the sitter in the Museo Grimani portrait, and not that in the Schorr painting, is actually Giovanni Grimani.
19 Boschloo, Van der Sman 1993, pp. 90–91, no. 87.
20 Gronau 1929; Bercken 1942, p. 103.
21 Pallucchini 1983, p. 184.
22 Venturi 1927, p. 296: "sovrana potenza del modellato nella testa sanguigna e angolosa, con occhi brillanti, acuti, di un grigio acciaio."
23 It has been noted, however, that "the indistinct execution of the cardinal red cape might indicate the hand of a collaborator" (Boschloo, Van der Sman 1993, p. 90).
24 The same occurred with the painting in the Riijksmuseum, Amsterdam. The author, instead, examined the panel in private collection directly and from close distance.
25 Paschini 1957; see also Laven 1967, Del Col 2008, Benzoni, Bortolotti 2002, Firpo 2010.
26 Grendler 1977, p. 32,
27 Laven 1967, p. 187; Ferrari 2021, p. 131.
28 Paul 2018, p. 34.
29 Ballarin 2017.
30 Pallucchini 1983, p. 184.
31 Firpo 2010, p. 157.
32 Benzoni, Bortolotti 2002.
33 On Paschini's hypothesis, see Benzoni, Bortolotti 2002.
34 This aspect is discussed in further detail in the present volume by Francesco Trentini.
35 Firpo 2010, p. 156.
36 Firpo 2010, p. 158.
37 Paschini 1957, pp. 190–91; Firpo 2010, pp. 143, 146, 148.
38 On this campaign and Grimani's actual involvement in it, see Francesco Trentini's essay in this volume.

Paolini da Udine 1593
F. Paolini da Udine, *In funere illustrissimi et reverendissimi Ioannis Grimani patriarchae aquieleinsis oratio in D. Marci aede III non. Oct. MDXCIII ex tempore habita a Fabio Paulino Utinensi philosopho, ac medico, graecarumque literarum publco doctore ad serenissimum Senatum venetum qui interfuit*, Venice: Giorgio Angelerio, 1593

Deciani 1602
T. Deciani, *Responsorium clarissimi ac celeberrimi i. v. consultissimi Tiberii Deciani...*, I, Venice: Vassallino, 1602

Moschini 1815
G. Moschini, *Guida per la città di Venezia all'amico delle belle arti*, Venice: tipografia Alvisopoli, 1815

[Moschini] n.d. [1819]
[G. Moschini], *Courte description des choses plus remarquables du Palais Grimani a Sainte Maria Formosa*, Venice: n.n., n.d. [1819]

Moschini 1828
G. Moschini, *Nuova guida per Venezia con 45 oggetti di arti incisi e un compendio della Istoria veneziana*, Venice: tipografia Alvisopoli, 1828

Waagen 1854
G. F. Waagen, *Treasures of Art in Great Britain*, London: John Murray, 1854, II, p. 177

Biermann 1927
G. Biermann, "Ein Tintoretto Porträt," in *Der Cicerone* no. 19, 1927, pp. 704–05

Venturi 1927
A. Venturi, *Studi dal vero attraverso le raccolte artistiche d'Europa*, Milan: Hoepli, 1927

Gronau 1929
H. D. Gronau, "Zu Tintoretto's Porträt im Rijksmuseum," in *Pantheon* no. 4, November 1929, p. LV

Vivian Neal 1939
A. W. Vivian Neal, C. M. Vivian Neal, "Cardinal Marino Grimani," in *Poundisford Park. A catalogue of Pictures and Furniture*, Taunton: The Wessex Press, 1939, no. 70, pp. 35–36

Bercken 1942
E. von der Bercken, *Die Gemälde des Jacopo Tintoretto*, Munich: Piper, 1942

Colnaghi 1947
"Jacopo Robusti, called Tintoretto (1518–1594). A cardinal of the Grimani Family," in *Catalogue of Paintings by Old Masters: November–December 1947*, London: P. & D. Colnaghi & Co, 1947, p. XX

Paschini 1956
P. Paschini, "Il mecenatismo artistico del patriarca Giovanni Grimani," in *Studi in onore di Aristide Calderini e Roberto Paribeni*, vol. 3, Milan: Ceschina, 1956, pp. 851–62

Berenson 1957
B. Berenson, *Italian pictures of the Renaissance: Venetian School*, London: Phaidon, 1957, p. 174

Paschini 1957
P. Paschini, *Tre illustri prelati del Rinascimento: Ermolao Barbaro, Adriano Castellesi, Giovanni Grimani*, Rome: Facultas theologica Pontificii Athenaei Lateranensis, 1957

Laven 1967
P. J. Laven, "The Causa Grimani and its Political Overtones," in *Journal of Religious History* vol. 4, no. 3, 1967, pp. 184–205

Pallucchini 1969
R. Pallucchini, *Tiziano*, Florence: Sansoni, 1969

Castelnuovo 1973
E. Castelnuovo, "Il significato del ritratto pittorico nella società," in *Storia d'Italia. V: i documenti*, Turin: Einaudi, 1973, pp. 1033–94

Rossi 1973
P. Rossi, *Jacopo Tintoretto*, vol. I, *I ritratti*, Venice: Alfieri 1973

Grendler 1977
P. F. Grendler, *The Roman Inquisition and the Venetian Press, 1540–1605*, Princeton, NJ: Princeton University Press, 1977

Foscari, Tafuri 1983
A. Foscari, M. Tafuri, *L'armonia e i conflitti. La chiesa di San Francesco della Vigna nella Venezia del '500*, Turin: Einaudi, 1983

Pallucchini 1983
R. Pallucchini, "Un nuovo ritratto di Jacopo Tintoretto," in *Arte Veneta* no. 37, 1983, pp. 184–87

Shearman 1983
J. Shearman, *The Early Italian Pictures in the Collection of Her Majesty the Queen*, Cambridge: Cambridge University Press, 1983

Pin 1985
Venezia, il Patriarcato di Aquileia e le "Giurisdizioni nelle terre patriarcali del Friuli" (1420–1620). Trattato inedito di fra Paolo Sarpi, ed. by C. Pin, Udine: Deputazione di storia patria per il Friuli, 1985

Firpo, Marcatto 1988
I processi inquisitoriali di Pietro Carnesecchi, 1557–1567, ed. by M. Firpo and D. Marcatto, Città del Vaticano: Archivio segreto vaticano, 1988

Cieri Via 1989
C. Cieri Via, "L'immagine del ritratto. Considerazioni sull'origine del genere e sulla sua evoluzione dal Quattrocento al Cinquecento," in *Il ritratto e la memoria. Materiali I*, ed. by A. Gentili, Rome: Bulzoni, 1989, pp. 45–91

Boschloo, Van der Sman 1993
Italian Paintings from the Sixteenth Century in Dutch Public Collections, ed. by A. W. Boschloo and G. J. van der Sman, Florence: Centro Di, 1993

Favaretto 1993
I. Favaretto, "Collezioni di antichità a Venezia nel Cinquecento e la formazione dello Statuario Pubblico," in *Tesori di scultura greca a Venezia*, ed. by I. Favaretto, G. Traversari, Venice: Cartotecnica veneziana, 1993, pp. 11–34

Tafuri 1994 (
M. Tafuri, "Il pubblico e il privato. Architettura e committenza a Venezia," in *Storia di Venezia dalle origini alla caduta della Serenissima*, ed. by G. Cozzi and P. Prodi, vol. VI, Rome: Istituto della Enciclopedia Italiana, 1994, pp. 367–477

Favaretto, Ravagnan 1997
Lo Statuario Pubblico della Serenissima. Due secoli di collezionismo di antichità 1596–1797, ed. by I. Favaretto, G. L. Ravagnan, Cittadella (PD): Biblos, 1997

Voltolina 1998
P. Voltolina, *La storia di Venezia attraverso le medaglie*, Venice: Edizioni Voltolina, 1998

Bristot 2000
A. Bristot, "Le decorazioni a stucco di Giovanni da Udine nel Palazzo veneziano dei Grimani di Santa Maria Formosa e il loro restauro," in *L'arte dello stucco in Friuli nei secoli XVII–XVIII*, conference proceedings, Udine: Udine Musei, 2000, pp. 93–104

Bristot 2001
A. Bristot, "Dedicato all'amore per l'antico: il camerino di Apollo a palazzo Grimani," in *Arte Veneta* no. 58, 2001, pp. 42–93

Craievich 2001
A. Craievich, "Una proposta per la "Psiche" di Francesco Salviati a palazzo Grimani, in *Arte Veneta* no.58, 2001, pp. 95–109

Hochmann 2001
M. Hochmann, "Les collections des familles "papalistes" à Venise et à Rome du XVIe au XVIIIe siècle," in *Geografia del collezionismo. Italia e Francia tra il XVI e il XVIII secolo*, seminar proceedings (Rome, École Française de Rome, 19–21 September 1996), ed. by O. Bonfait *et al.*, Rome: École Française de Rome, 2001, pp. 203–23

Benzoni, Bortolotti 2002
G. Benzoni, L. Bortolotti, "Grimani Giovanni," in *Dizionario Biografico degli Italiani*, vol. LIX, Rome: Istituto della Enciclopedia Italiana, 2002, pp. 613–21

Soccal 2002
E. Soccal, "Sculture antiche a Venezia nel Cinquecento: Palazzo Grimani e il suo museo. I. La Tribuna nel XVI secolo. Proposte per una lettura del programma iconografico," in *Iconografia 2001. Studi sull'immagine*, conference proceedings (Padua, 30 May – 1 June 2001), ed. by I. Colpo and I. Favaretto, Rome: Quasar, 2002, pp. 447–55

Cavina 2004
M. Cavina, *Tiberio Deciani (1509–1582). Alle origini del pensiero giuridico moderno*, Udine: Forum, 2004

Christie's 2004
Christie's, London, *Studio of Jacopo Tintoretto, Portrait of a Cardinal, thought to be Cardinal Giovanni Grimani*, 21 April 2004, lot 92 (https://www.christies.com/lot/lot-4266337?ldp_breadcrumb=back&intObjectID=4266337&from=salessummary&lid=1)

Favaretto 2004
I. Favaretto, "Un 'cortile delle statue' veneziano. Per un percorso della memoria nel palazzo dei Grimani di Santa Maria Formosa," in *Studi in onore di G. Traversari*, ed. by M. Fano Santi, vol. I, Rome: L'Erma di Bretschneider, 2004, pp. 341–61

Firpo 2005
M. Firpo, "L'iconografia come problema storiografico. Le ambiguità della porpora e i "diavoli" del Sant'Ufficio. Identità e storia nei ritratti di Giovanni Grimani," in *Rivista storica italiana* vol. CXVII, no. 3, 2005, pp. 825–71

De Paoli 2006–2007
M. De Paoli, "Intorno a palazzo Grimani e alle sue raccolte di antichità. Le sculture del cortile, i vasi e i bronzi del primo piano," in *Atti dell'Istituto Veneto di Scienze Lettere ed Arti* no. CLXV, 2006–2007, pp. 419–59

Ferrara 2008
F. Ferrara, "Il busto in bronzo di Antonio Grimani. Ipotesi sull'attribuzione e sui contesti," in *L'industria artistica del bronzo nel Rinascimento a Venezia e nell'Italia settentrionale*, proceedings of the international study conference (Venice, Fondazione Giorgio Cini, 23–24 October 2007), ed. by M. Ceriana and V. Avery, Verona: Scripta, 2008, pp. 157–77

Puppi 2007
L. Puppi, "*Ritratto del Patriarca Giovanni Grimani,* scheda n. 118," in *Tiziano: l'ultimo atto*, exhibition catalogue (Belluno, Palazzo Crepadona, 15 September 2007 – 6 January 2008), ed. by L. Puppi, Milan: Skira, 2007, pp. 422–23

Del Col 2008
A. Del Col, "Le vicende inquisitoriali di Giovanni Grimani, patriarca di Aquileia, e la sua lettera sulla doppia predestinazione," in *Metodi e Ricerche* no. 27, 2008, pp. 81–100

Pancheri 2009
R. Pancheri, "scheda 75. Bottega di Domenico Tintoretto (?), *Ritratto del patriarca di Aquileia Giovanni Grimani*," in *L'uomo del Concilio. Il cardinale Giovanni Morone tra Roma e Trento nell'età di Michelangelo*, exhibition catalogue (Trento, 4 April – 26 July 2009), ed. by R. Pancheri and D. Primerano, technical consulting M. Firpo, Trento: Temi, 2009, pp. 311–13

Buccheri 2010
A. Buccheri, "Il Ritratto. Storia e funzione di un genere artistico," in *L'arte e il visuale*, vol. X, Enciclopedia della cultura italiana, 10 voll., Turin: UTET, 2010, pp. 337–74

Firpo 2010
M. Firpo, "Le ambiguità della porpora e i "diavoli" del Sant'Ufficio: identità e storia nei ritratti di Giovanni Grimani," in M. Firpo, *Storie di immagini, immagini di storia. Studi di iconografia cinquecentesca*, Rome: Edizioni di Storia e Letteratura, 2010, pp. 119–71 (155, fig. 45 a p. 150), already published in *Rivista Storica Italiana* vol. CXVII, no. 3, 2005, pp. 825–71

Davis 2011
"East of Italy: early documentation of Mediterranean Antiquities, excerpts from Sebastiano Serlio: *Il terzo libro di Sebastiano Serlio Bolognese nel qual si figurano e descrivono le antiquità di Roma, e le altre cose che sono in Italia, e fuori d'Italia* (Venezia 1540)," ed. by M.D. Davis, in *Fontes. Quellen und Dokumente zur Kunst 1350–1750* no. 57, 2011, p.n.n.

Favaretto, De Paoli 2011
I. Favaretto, M. De Paoli, "La tribuna ritrovata. Uno schizzo inedito di Federico Zuccari con l'antiquario dell'Ill. patriarca Grimani," in *Eidola* no. 7, 2010–2011, pp. 97–135

De Paoli 2012
M. De Paoli, "*Vicinaque sidere me fecit*. La stanza di Callisto a Palazzo Grimani," in *Il gran poema delle passioni e delle meraviglie*, ed. by I. Colpo and F. Ghedini, Padua: Padova University Press, 2012, pp. 319–30

Zugno, 2012–2013
F. Zugno, *Decorazioni naturalistiche nella Venezia del '500: la sala a fogliami di Palazzo Grimani e la sacrestia di San Salvador*, Italian M.A. dissertation, Università Ca' Foscari Venezia, professor M. Frank, academic year 2012–2013

Hochmann 2014
M. Hochmann, "Un fregio di Palma il Giovane a palazzo Grimani di San Luca," in *Artibus et Historiae*, vol. 35, no. 70, 2014, pp. 157–69, fig. 4.

Furlan 2014
C. Furlan, "Domenico, Marino e Giovanni Grimani tra passione per l'antico, gusto del collezionismo e mecenatismo artistico," in *I cardinali della Serenissima. Arte e committenza tra Venezia e Roma*, ed. by C. Furlan, Cinisello Balsamo (MI): Silvana Editoriale, 2014, pp. 31–73

Samperi 2014
R. Samperi, "La vigna Grimani 'in Monte Caballi': reddito e prestigio," in *I cardinali della Serenissima. Arte e committenza tra Venezia e Roma*, ed. by C. Furlan, Cinisello Balsamo (MI): Silvana Editoriale, 2014, pp. 367–87

Wright 2014
C. Wright, *The Schorr Collection: Catalogue of Old Master and Nineteenth-Century Paintings*, 2 vols., London: Marylebone and General Fine Art, 2014

Ballarin 2017
A. Ballarin, *Jacopo Tintoretto: ritratto del Cardinale Marcantonio da Mula*, Florence: De Stijl Art Publishing, 2017

Lempertz 2017
Lempertz, Köln, Domenico Tintoretto, *Portrait of Giovanni Grimani, Patriarch of Aquileia*, 18 November 2017, lot 2025: https://www.lempertz.com/en/catalogues/lot/1097-1/2025-domenico-tintoretto.html

Paul 2018
B. Paul, "Bad Colours for the Pope. Tintoretto, Giovanni Grimani and the Decoration of the Cappella Gregoriana in New St Peter's," in *Artistic Practices and Cultural Transfer in Early Modern Italy. Essays in Honour of Deborah Howard*, ed. by N. Avcioğlu and A. Sherman, London: Routledge, 2018, pp. 29–43

Bravetti 2019
G. Bravetti, *Per una storia degli studi italiani sul ritratto. Alcune riflessioni, La fantasia e la storia. Studi di Storia dell'arte sul ritratto dal Medioevo al contemporaneo*, ed. by G. Brevetti, Palermo: Palermo University Press, 2019, pp. 7–35

Trentini 2019
F. Trentini, "Etologia e metafora del mondo nella Sala a fogliami di Palazzo Grimani," in *Animali figurati*, ed. by S. Riccioni e L. Perissinotto, Rome: Viella, 2019, pp. 267–90

Venetian Heritage 2020
Ritratto del patriarca Giovanni Grimani, Domenico Tintoretto (attr.), inizio XVII secolo, Museo di Palazzo Grimani, Venezia: https://https://www.venetianheritage.eu/it/portfolio/ritratto-del-patriarca-giovanni-grimani-domenico-tintoretto-attr-inizio-xvii-secolo/

Wolters 2020
W. Wolters, *Palazzo Grimani a Santa Maria Formosa: osservazioni e ipotesi*, in *Dilettanti di architettura nella Venezia del Cinquecento*, seminar proceedings (Venice, Istituto Veneto di Scienze, Lettere ed Arti, 2020), ed. by M. Gaier and W. Wolters, Venice: Istituto Veneto di Scienze, Lettere ed Arti, 2020, pp. 77–93

Ferrara, Bergamo Rossi 2021
D. Ferrara, T. Bergamo Rossi, *"Domus Grimani. 1594–2019". The Collection of Classical Sculptures Reassembled in its Original Setting after Four Centuries*, Venice: Marsilio, 2021

Ferrari 2021
S. Ferrari, *The Role of Cardinals' Portraits in Venice. The Case of the Grimani Family and Some Thoughts on the Correr MS Morosini Grimani 270*, in *Portrait Cultures of the Early Modern Cardinal*, ed. by P. Baker-Bates and I. Brooke, Amsterdam: Amsterdam University Press, 2021, pp. 117–48

Hochmann 2021
M. Hochmann, "A propos du Portrait de Zuan Zulian à la National Gallery: Une œuvre d'Antonio Boselli?," in *Close Reading, in Kunsthistorische Interpretationen vom Mittelalter bis in die Moderne. Festschrift für Sebastian Schütze*, ed. by S. Albl, B. Hub, and A. Frasca-Rath, Berlin–Boston: De Gruyter, 2021, pp. 122–29

Mallamace 2021–2022
G. Mallamace, *Et le scale di sopra lavorate di pittura e di stucchi. Rinnovate riflessioni sullo scalone monumentale di Palazzo Grimani a Santa Maria Formosa*, Italian M.A. dissertation, Università Ca' Foscari Venezia, professor V. Sapienza, academic year 2021–2022

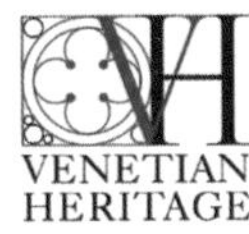

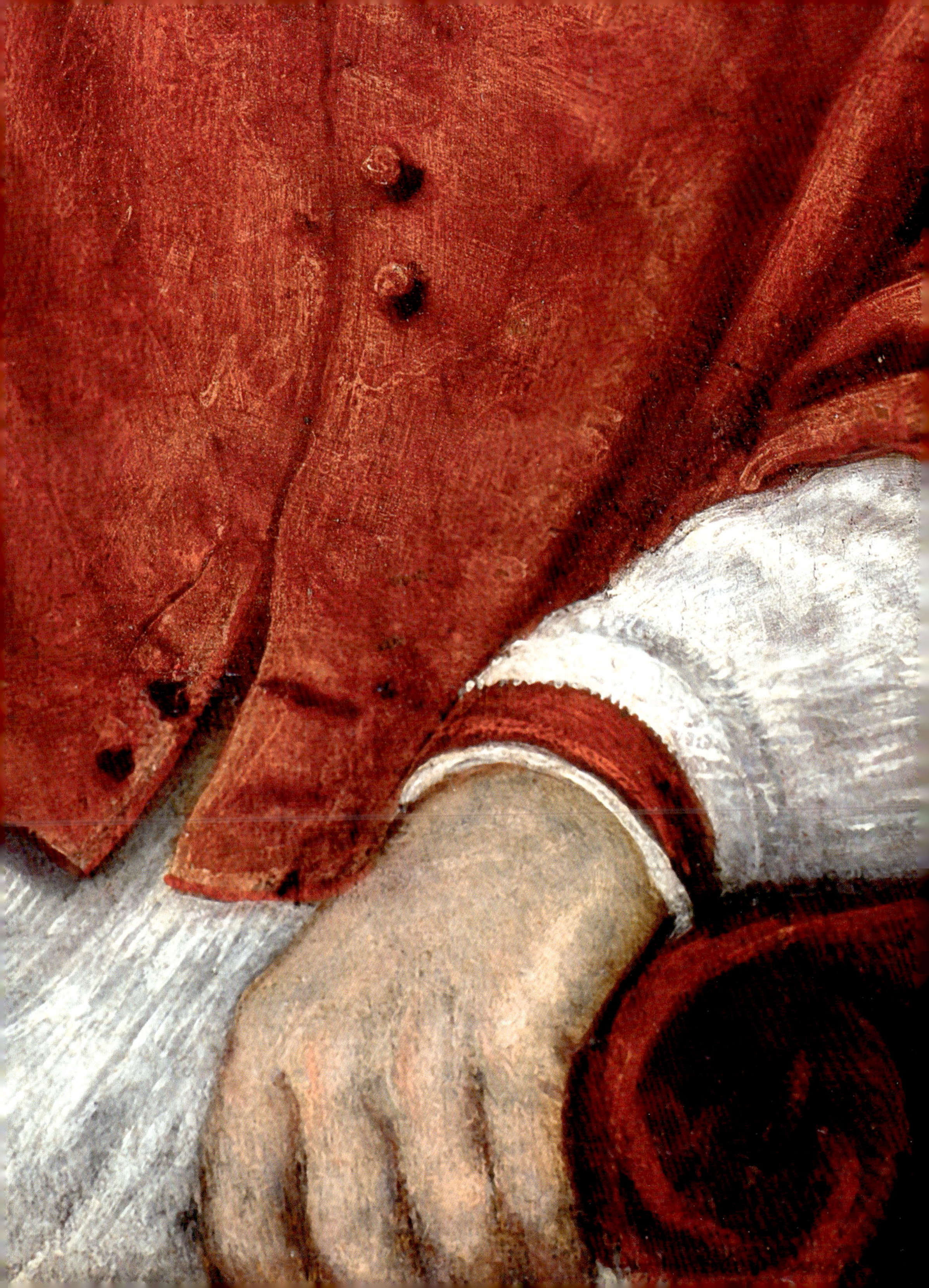

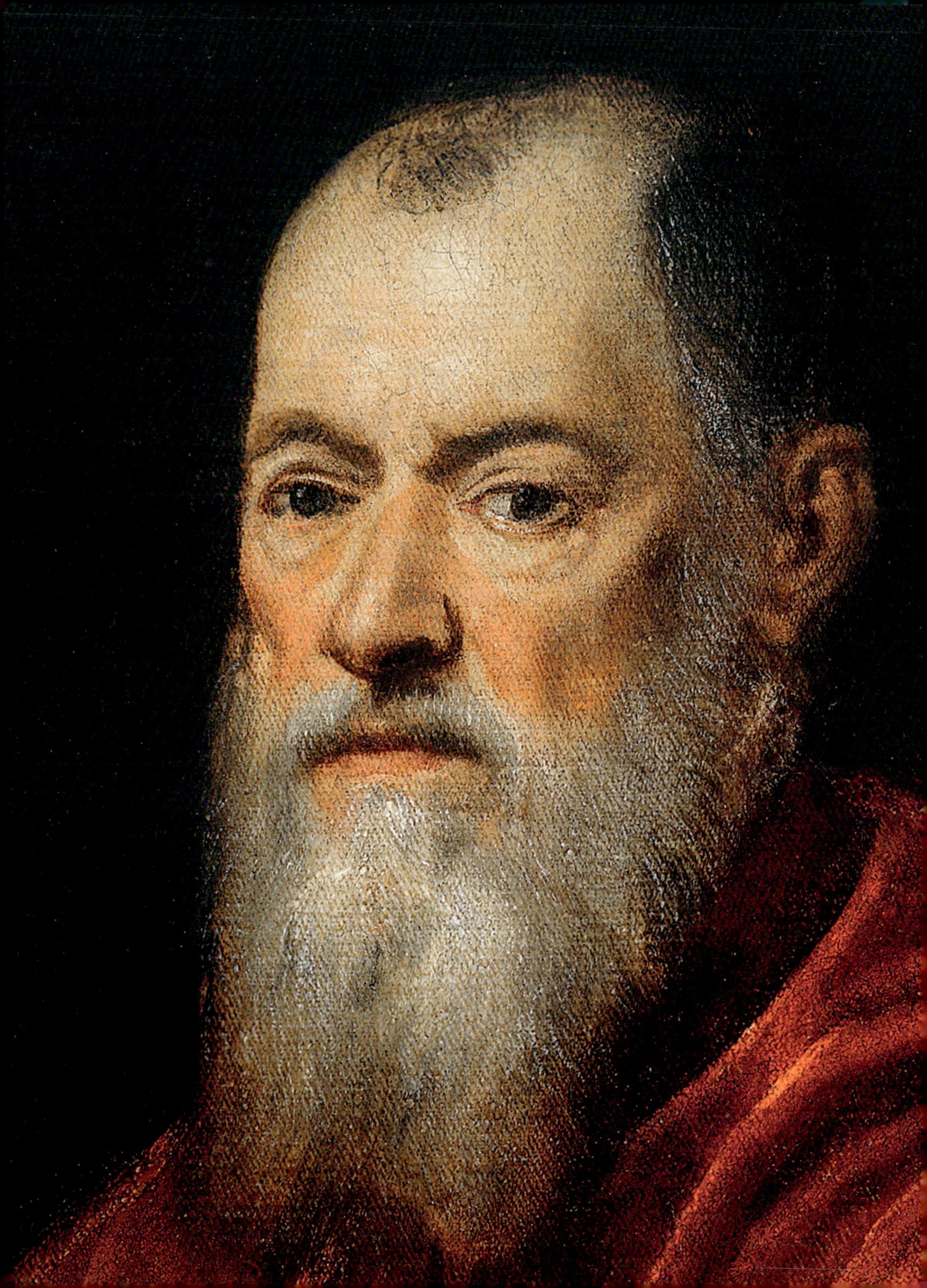

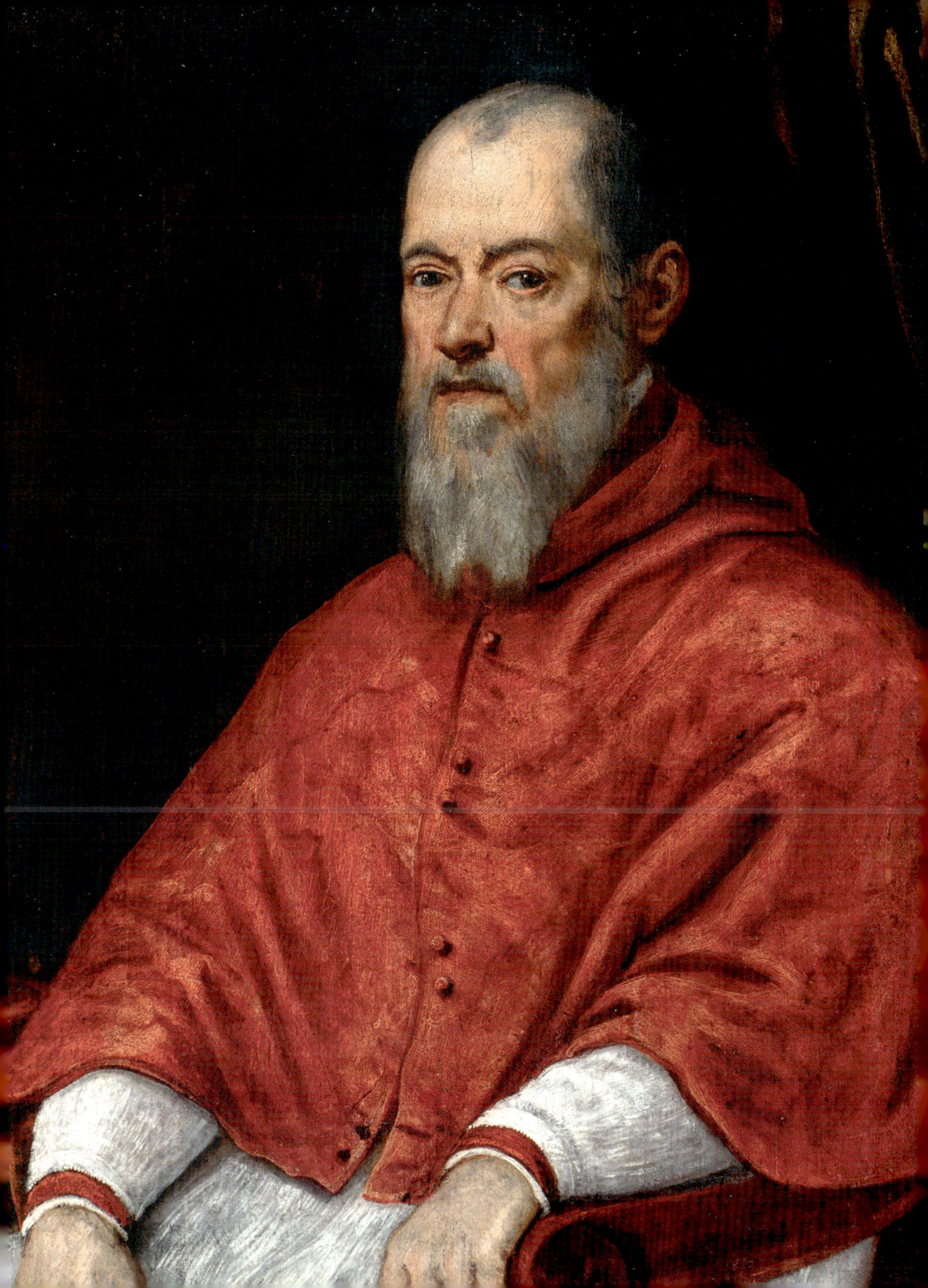

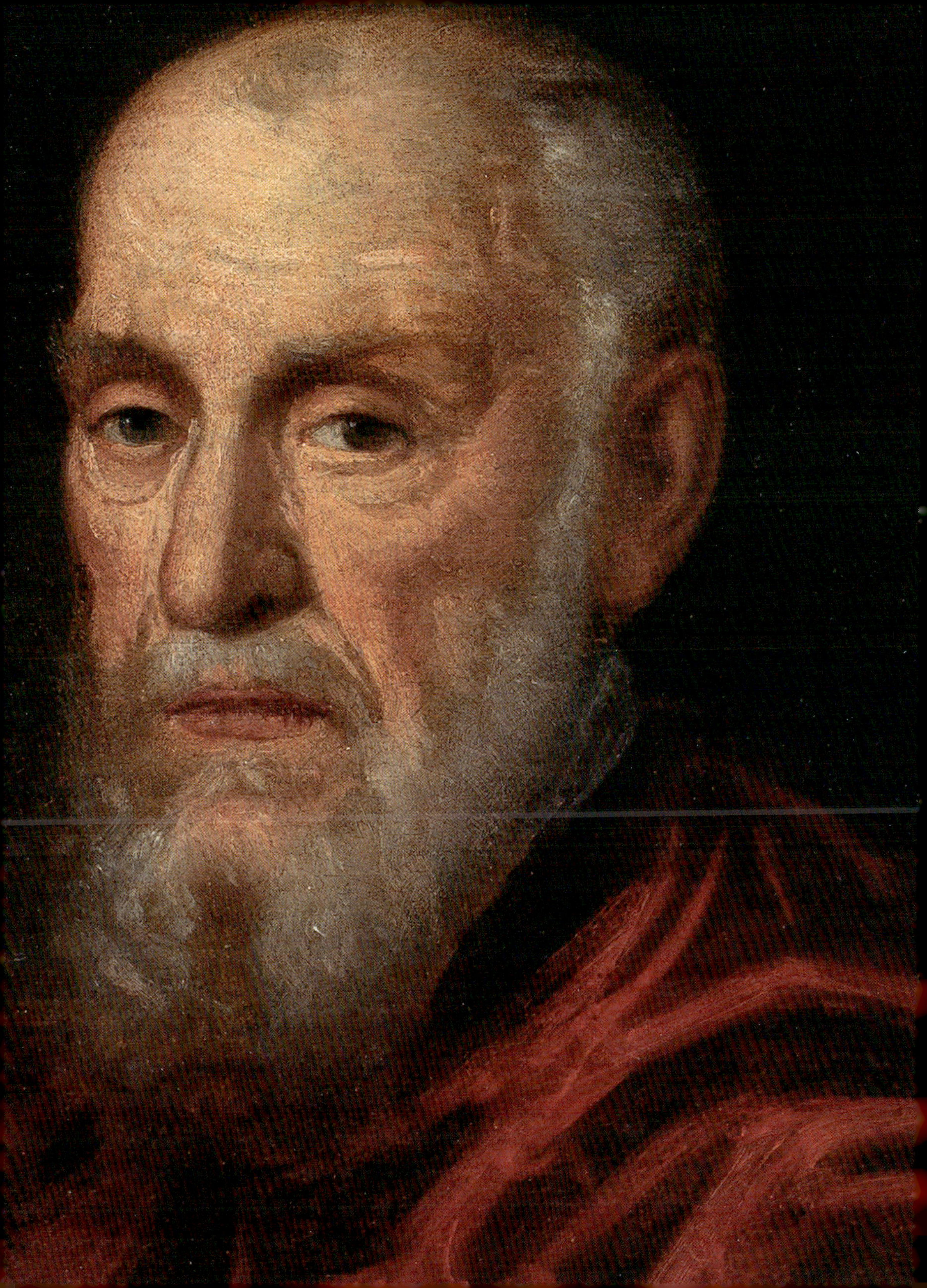

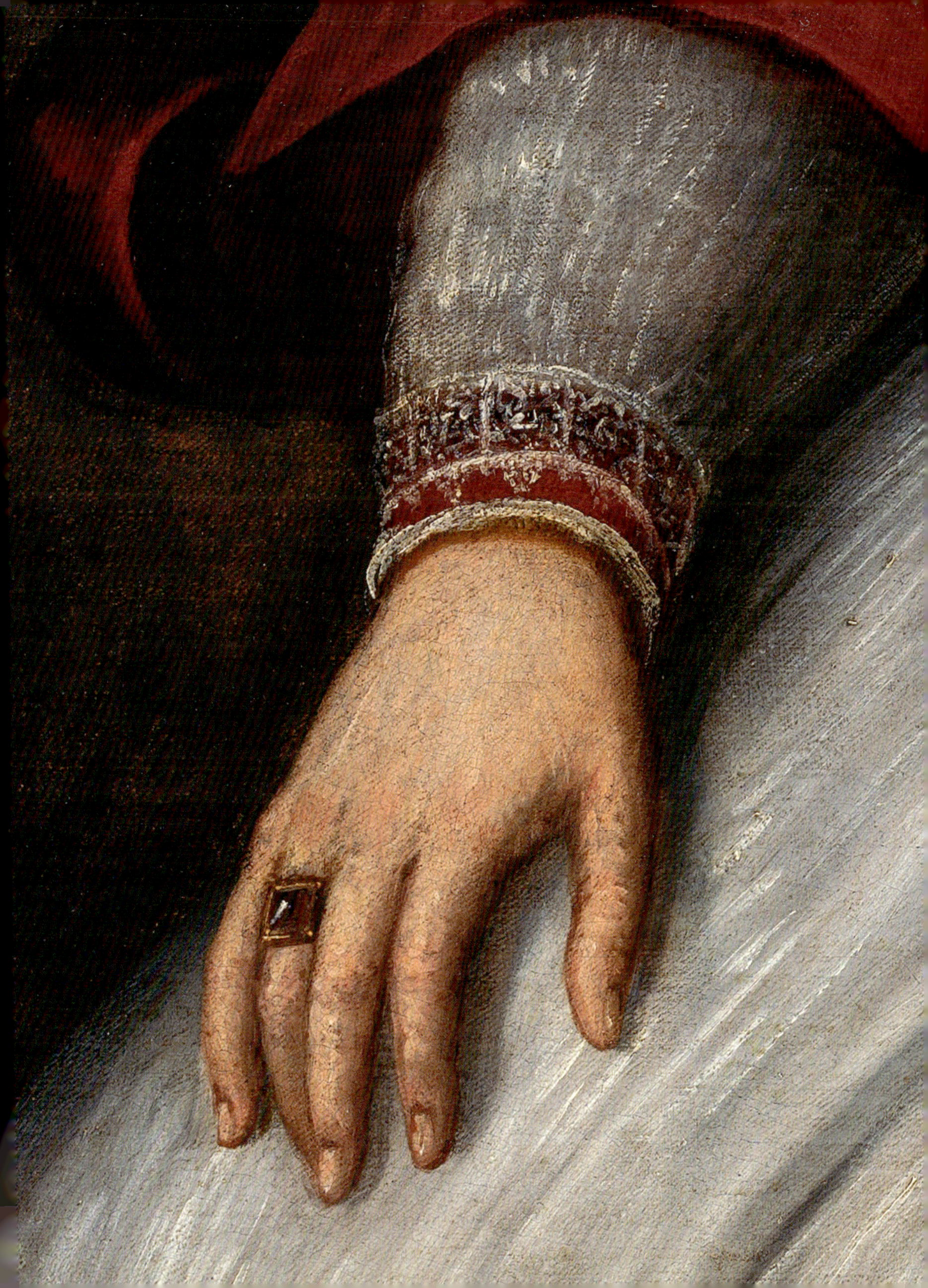

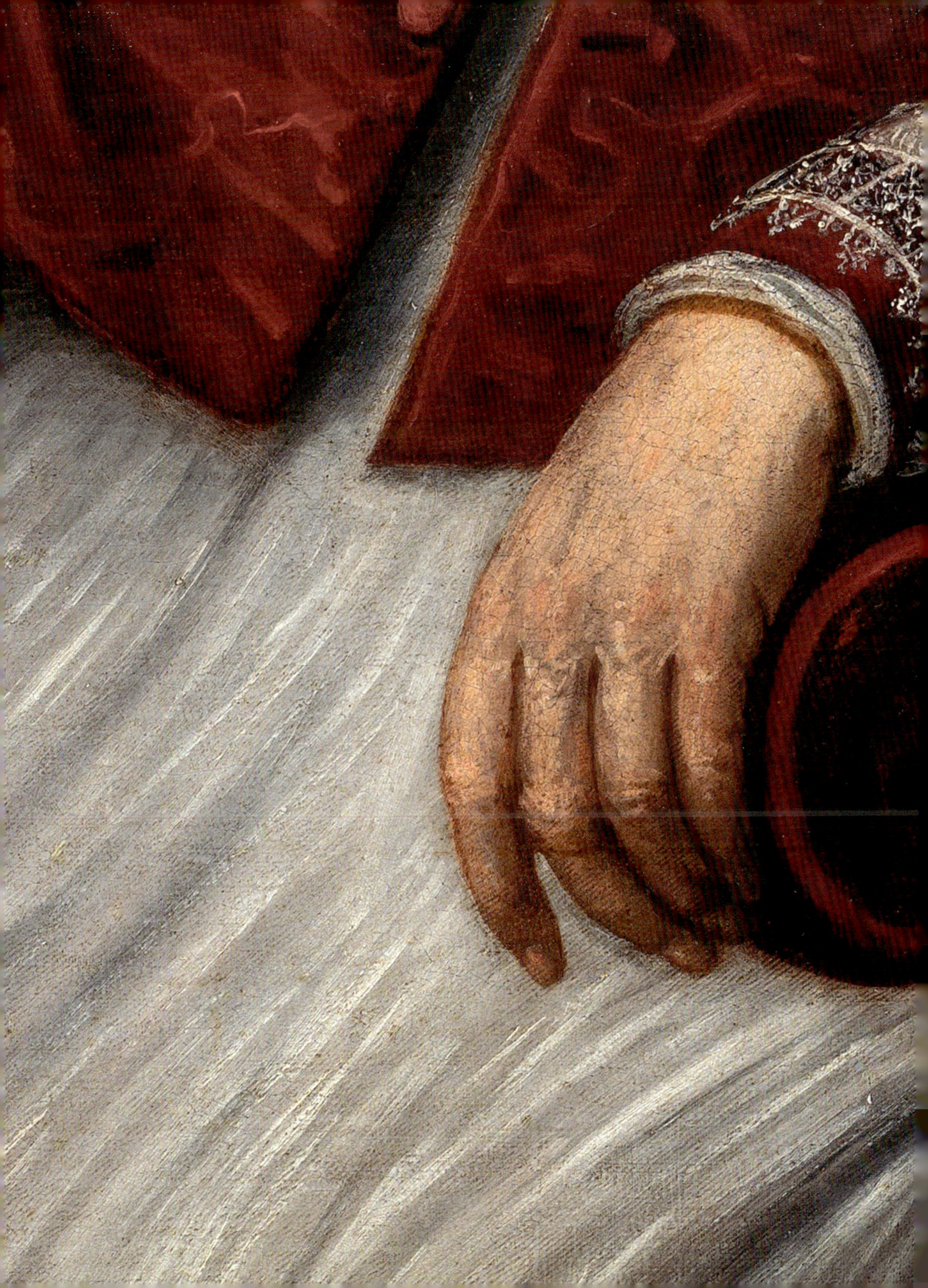

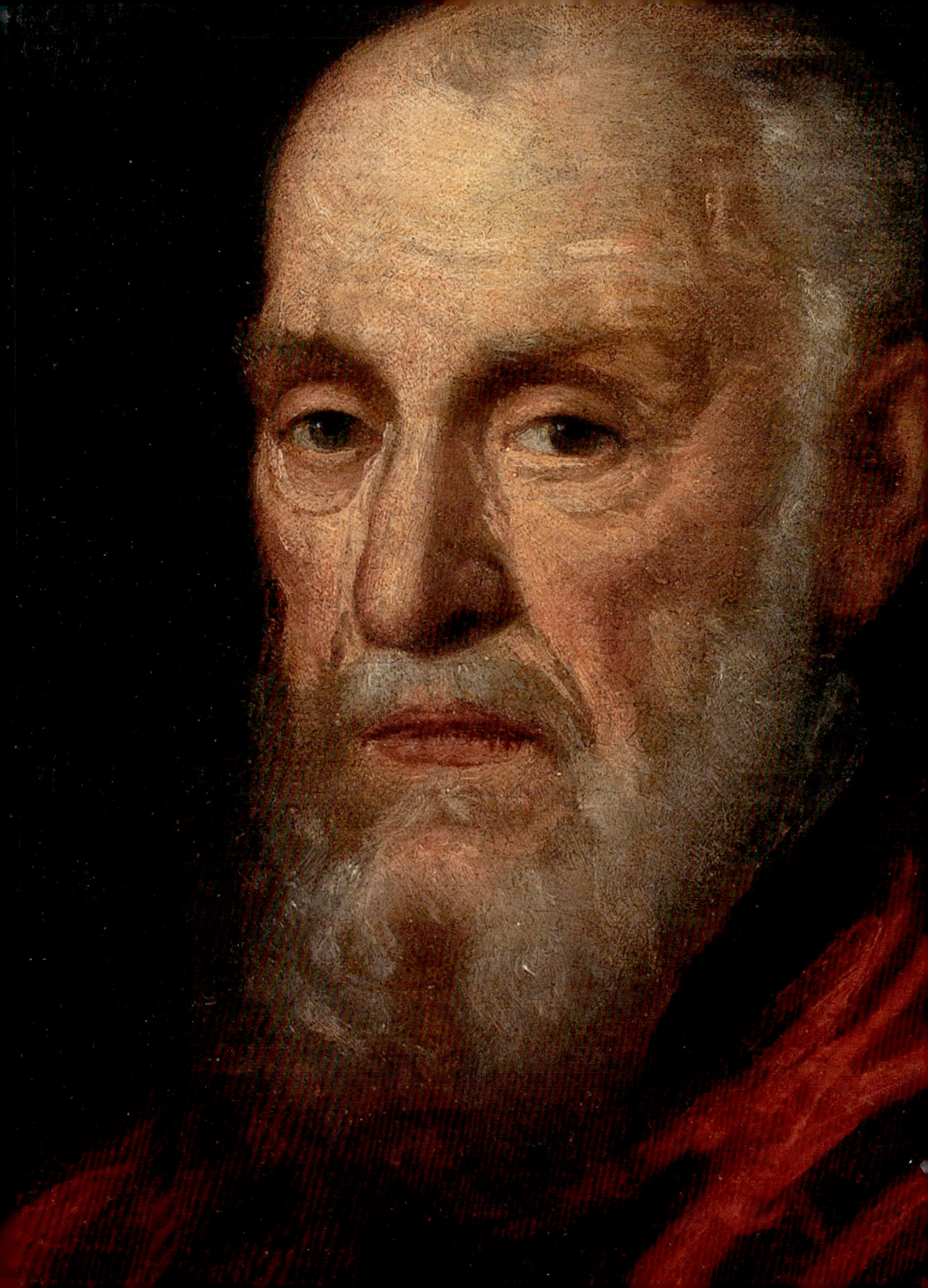